A Prince to

Charles Stokes Wayne

Alpha Editions

This edition published in 2024

ISBN 9789362093615

Design and Setting By
Alpha Editions
www.alphaedis.com
Email - info@alphaedis.com

As per information held with us this book is in Public Domain. This book is a reproduction of an important historical work. Alpha Editions uses the best technology to reproduce historical work in the same manner it was first published to preserve its original nature. Any marks or number seen are left intentionally to preserve.

Contents

I	- 1 -
II	- 10 -
III	- 16 -
IV	- 24 -
V	- 33 -
VI	- 42 -
VII	- 53 -
VIII	- 60 -
IX	- 71 -
X	- 81 -
XI	- 88 -
XII	- 97 -
XIII	- 105 -
XIV	- 113 -
XV	- 121 -
XVI	- 127 -
XVII	- 135 -
XVIII	- 144 -
XIX	- 150 -
XX	- 157 -
XXI	- 165 -

I

GREY'S awakening was as gradual as a clouded dawn. For a time dreams and realities intermingled. Then slowly a partial consciousness of his physical being obtruded: his fingers were clutching a silken coverlet; he turned on his side and the linen pillow-case was cool to his cheek; through half-open eyelids a sweep of pale blue became visible. Later he realised that he was in a curtained bed and that the blue was the colour of the draperies. He lay still for a long while—drowsy, inert, his sensibilities numb. Presently the ticking of a clock became audible, and then a rumble of street sounds. At the same moment a throbbing pain in his head asserted itself. With an effort he sat up, his hands pressed against his temples, his mind groping. Then in a flash the unfamiliarity of his surroundings aroused him suddenly, sharply, like a cold plunge, and his brain cleared a trifle. His memory went staggering back after the night before; but the mists descended again and the way grew dark, and he could remember no night without its morning.

He put his feet to the floor and stood up, but a dizziness overcame him, and he sank back upon the bed, weak and limp. His heart was beating tumultuously and his breath came in short, quick gasps. After a little these abnormalities passed and he raised himself on one elbow, resting his cheek on his hand. At the contact he started, amazed, bewildered. In some unaccountable manner he had grown a beard. His hand ran from his cheek to his chin. Close-cropped at the sides it was here an inch long and trimmed to a point, and his moustache was one of several months' culture and training. He fancied he was dreaming and would awaken presently to find himself clean-shaven, as he had been for years.

And now, he remembered; after all, it was quite clear. He had been to the opera last night, had gone from there to the club, had returned home late, and, having a pressing business appointment at ten this morning, had dragged himself out of bed at eight, still fagged and aggravatingly sleepy. Now he had just had his coffee, and while Lutz was shaving him he was dozing and dreaming.

But how wonderfully real the transformation all seemed! He grew curious as to how he looked with beard and moustache, and, crawling out between the pale-blue velvet curtains, he sought a mirror. The revelation was dumfounding. He, Carey Grey, who from infancy had been as dark as a Spaniard, was as blond as a Norseman. He ran his fingers through his hair, tousled it, going closer to the glass to make sure that there was not some optical illusion. He puffed out his lip and pulled at his moustache until his lowered eyes could see it, and he thrust his chin forward and turned up the point of his beard with the back of his hand until it, too, came within the range of his vision. If this were a dream, he told himself, never before had dream been so real. If it were a reality, never before had reality been so mystifying.

His puzzled survey of himself was followed by a minute inspection of the room into which he had been so mysteriously transported. Its general aspect was foreign; its detail distinctly French. The walls were panelled and medallioned. The bed from which he had risen was one of a pair, each with its gilded *papier mâché* frieze and its looped-back blue velvet curtains. At the head of each bed were six pillows and another of down at the foot. The full-length mirror into which he had gazed was duplicated between two windows. Upon the mantel was a bronze and gilt clock, flanked by partially burned candles in brass sticks. Two tables, a couch, a washstand, a cheffonier, three chairs and a wardrobe completed the furnishing. A couple of companion pictures, unmistakably French both in conception and execution, decorated two of the wall panels. The hands of the clock stood at twenty minutes of four. He crossed to a window with three sets of curtains and three sets of cord loops all of a tangle, and looked out.

For the spectacle that confronted him he was not prepared. The change in his appearance had indeed been incomprehensible; the strangeness of the room in which he awakened was inexplicable; but to discover at a glance that he was no longer on his native soil, that without his knowledge he had been carried across sea and land and dropped into a Paris hotel on the Boulevard des Italiens, was not only inconceivable but terrifying. He was very pale, and his brain was reeling. Twice he drew trembling fingers across his eyes, as if to wipe out the kaleidoscope of the street below; but when he looked again the view was even more convincing. It was a bit of the French Capital with which he was almost as familiar as with that part of Fifth avenue lying within range of his club windows or with that portion of Broad street near Wall into which he had been wont to glance from his office in the Mills Building.

He turned away from it as from a nightmare, and, sitting down, tried to think. The idea that he was dreaming was not tenable. He knew that he was very wide awake and thoroughly possessed of his faculties. His head still ached with a dull, swollen, congested sensation such as follows a too riotous night, but he could recall nothing of the cause. It occurred to him now that he had read in the newspapers of cases where men had lost their memory for months and had wandered into remote states or countries. This must be the explanation. And in his aberration he had given way to some freak of fancy, had grown a beard and then had had it and his hair bleached corn colour. Men under similar mental derangement, he recollected, forgot their names and homes. Perhaps he had been in the same plight. Now, however, his mind was clear on those points, at least, and he thanked God for his restoration.

Then he wondered how long he had been away. That night at the opera and the club; that morning he had risen early to keep an engagement, and had dozed off while his valet was shaving him—why, that was midwinter; and now, if he could judge by the trees on the boulevard, and the tables in front of the Café Riche across the road, and the straw hats, it must be early summer—late May or June; possibly, indeed, July. And all this time his friends at home—his mother, his fiancée, his partner—were probably thinking him dead. What a relief it would be to them to get the cablegrams he would send, telling that he was alive and well and was returning by the first steamer!

He smiled as he got up and went to the cheffonier and the wardrobe in search of clothes. He was thinking of the sensation the papers in New York must have made over his disappearance; the theories they must have advanced and the pictures they must have published. And then the tragic side of the affair took hold of him, and he put himself in his mother's place, in Hope's place, and fancied he could appreciate, in a way at least, their anxiety as the days passed without tidings, and their grief and despair as weeks quadrupled into months.

Having discovered an assortment of garments, including a bathrobe of pongee silk, he looked about for a tub. Across the passage he found a bathroom, and a dip into cold water relieved his headache and balanced his nerves. When at length he was in attire which, while quite as unfamiliar as his yellow hair and beard, was nevertheless tasteful and well fitting, he emerged from his room, locked the door and started forth on a tour of investigation. His curiosity had grown with his dressing, enhanced, perhaps, by his failure to find in any drawer, closet, or pocket a scrap of writing or printing from which he could gain a clue concerning his recent past. His sole discovery indeed had been a wallet containing two fifty-franc notes and a trunk key.

A tall, round-faced *portier* in green livery smiled and bowed, rather obsequiously he thought, as he passed out through the wide portal into the boulevard. Then the commingled scent of asphalt and macadam and burning charcoal—that characteristically Parisian odour—smote his olfactories, and before his eyes was the afternoon panorama of the gayest of Paris thoroughfares. It was the newspaper hour, and a kiosk in front of the hotel was being besieged by a horde, each hungry for his favourite journal. Every man that passed had a paper in his hand or in his pocket. Some were reading as they walked. On the roadway carriages, *fiacres*, omnibuses were crowding, and Grey noted, with a sense of old friends returned, the varnished hats of the *cochers*. The chairs under the awnings of the cafés were filling, and the white-aproned waiters were coming and going with their inevitable bustle of trays and glasses.

At the corner of the rue St. Anne he crossed to the north side of the boulevard and turned into the rue Taitbout, in which, he remembered, there was a telegraph office, for he meant to lose no time in despatching his cables. As he picked his way through the narrow street the messages took form, and on reaching the office it was but the labour of a moment to put them on paper, poke them in through the little window and pay the stipulated toll. To his mother he wired:

Safe and well. Sailing first steamer. Hôtel Grammont.

And the others—one addressed to Hope Van Tuyl, East Sixty-fourth street, New York, and one to "Malgrey," the code name of the stock brokerage firm in which he was a junior partner—were similar.

Rejoining the throng of pedestrians on the boulevard, he sauntered leisurely towards the Avenue de l'Opéra, his mind still busy with conjectures.

The billboards in front of the Théâtre du Vaudeville caught his eye, but the attractions they announced made no impression. At the groups of idlers seated at little round tables before the Café Américain he scarcely glanced and his own unfamiliar reflection in the plate glass of the shop windows he failed utterly to recognise. He crossed the Place de l'Opéra without so much as turning his head, and halting at the far corner stepped in under the ample awning of the Café de la Paix and found a seat. Of the waiter who approached him he ordered a *mazagran* and some Egyptian cigarettes, and when they were brought he sat for some time, heedless of his surroundings, his brain racked with futile speculations.

"*Pardon, monsieur!*"

Someone in passing had inadvertently touched his foot and was apologising. Startled out of his reverie he looked up, and his face lighted. Instantly he was on his feet.

"Frothingham, by all that's good!" he exclaimed.

The other, tall, straight and swarthy, turned upon him a look in which mystification and suspicion fought for supremacy.

"Really," he said, coldly, "I—I don't remember ever having———"

"Of course, of course," Grey interrupted, not without some embarrassment, "I can quite understand that you shouldn't recognise me. You see, I—well, I'm Carey Grey."

Mr. Frothingham's demeanour showed no change.

"Carey Grey," he repeated, icily; "I used to know a Carey Grey in New York, a member of the Knickerbocker and the Union; but he was nearly as dark as I am, and besides—why, he's dead."

"If you don't mind sitting down a bit," Grey went on, as he staggered under the news of his own demise, "I'll try to explain. I'm Carey Grey, just the same—*the* Carey Grey, of the Knickerbocker and the Union, and I'm not dead."

Frothingham recognised his voice now, and mystification routed suspicion from the field. He took a chair and Grey sat down, too, with the marble-topped table between them.

"First and foremost," Grey began, "tell me what day of the month it is."

"The fourteenth."

"Of what?"

"Of June, of course."

"And of the week?"

"Thursday."

"Thanks. I hadn't the slightest idea."

Frothingham fancied the man had gone mad.

"The whole thing is most extraordinary," Grey went on, and then he proceeded to relate his afternoon's experience, while his listener preserved an interested but incredulous silence.

"Can't remember a blessed thing," the narrator concluded, "since that morning last winter—I suppose it was last winter. What year is this?"

He was told.

"Yes, it was last winter, then—January, if I'm not mistaken."

Frothingham looked thoughtful and counted back. He wondered whether it was insanity or drugs, or—cunning.

"You must have heard something of it," Grey went on, eagerly. "Did the newspapers say I was dead?"

"I think that was the ultimate conclusion."

"I suppose they searched for me?"

"Oh, yes, they searched. They followed up every clue. There were columns in the papers for days—yes, for weeks."

Grey sighed audibly.

"I can't understand it," he said, with something of distress in his voice; "I never thought my head was weak. To be sure, I'd been under rather a strain, with the market in the unsettled condition it was, but my memory was always clear enough. Why, I could give you the closing price and highest and lowest of about every active stock on the list, day after day, without an error of an eighth. By the way, do you know how things have been going in the Street? What's New York Central now—and St. Paul?"

"Really, I have lost track, Grey," replied Frothingham indifferently.

"I must get a Paris *Herald*," the man who had been out of the world for five months continued; "I'm the modern Rip Van Winkle. Thousands of things have happened—must have happened, and I'm in blank ignorance. I just cabled to New York—to Mallory, my partner, and——"

"You what!" exclaimed Frothingham, in amazement.

"Cabled to Mallory. You know him—Dick Mallory, my partner. He'll be surprised to hear I'm alive, I suppose."

"Good God, man!"

"What's the matter?"

The two sat staring at each other across the table, each a picture of sudden startled bewilderment.

"Then you really don't know?" Frothingham asked. "Oh, that's impossible! You can't make me believe—see here, Carey, you're very clever and all that, but you don't think for one minute, do you, that you are taking me in? I did fancy for a little while that you'd gone off your head; but I was wrong. You're sharp and shrewd, and you feared I had recognised you and that that was why I stumbled over your foot; so you made up your mind that you'd block my game by recognising me and telling me this pipe dream. Oh, come, come, be fair! You know; and you know that I know."

Grey caught his breath sharply as this torrent of insult surged upon him. The blood rushed to his face only to desert it. His fists doubled instinctively, and he rose to his feet, white with indignant anger.

"Take that back!" he commanded, in a hoarse whisper. "Take it back, I say, or I'll——"

There was no mistaking his earnestness, his determination; no, nor at this juncture, his honesty. Frothingham was convinced even against his judgment.

"Oh, I say," he retorted, mildly, "don't make a scene, old chap. If I said anything, I—I—well, of course you don't understand. I see it now. I'm sure I was wrong, and I ask your pardon. There now, sit down."

"I don't know that I care to," Grey replied, the words of the other still rankling. "I'm not used to being called a blackguard. I've never in my life done anything to be seriously ashamed of, and nobody has ever dared, until this day, to utter such an insinuation."

Frothingham was silent for a moment, the mere suggestion of a smile on his lips. He calmly unbuttoned one of his gloves and then buttoned it again.

"God forbid," he said, without looking up, "that I should be the first to imply anything; but—I wish you would sit down, Grey!—you say you've lost count for five months, and—well, there are some things that you ought to know."

Grey resumed his seat. Now the man was talking reasonably. Of course there were things that he ought to know—hundreds of things probably in which he was personally interested. The thought instantly became appalling. What, indeed, might not have happened in five months? Where had he been during that time? And what had he been doing?

"Yes," he admitted, "you are quite right, I suppose. One of the things, for instance, is——"

"One of the things, for instance, is," repeated the other, interrupting him, "that you left New York suddenly—disappeared totally and—you ought to know this for your own salvation—under a cloud."

Grey started, and the colour that had returned to his face fled again. He leaned across the table, resting his arms on its marble top.

"Under a cloud!" he exclaimed, breathlessly. "My God, Frothingham! What do you mean?"

"I'd rather not go into details," was the answer, given very quietly. "It's not a pleasant position that I have chosen for myself, and I prefer that you don't question me. What you have told me—and I'm satisfied now it is the truth—has put another light on the whole business. And you really cabled to New York?"

"Not half an hour ago. I sent three."

"It's too late, I suppose, to stop them."

"I fancy so."

"I'd see, if I were you. It is important."

"But why? For God's sake, man, tell me why."

"No," said Frothingham, rising; "you'd better read about it for yourself. It will be more satisfactory. You can find a file of the New York *Herald* at the office of the Paris paper. It's only a block or so away, you know. Look up last January. But I'd try to stop those cables first. I must be off now; I've got an appointment." And he joined the now much augmented throng on the promenade.

Grey dropped a five-franc piece on the table, and hurried into a *fiacre* that stood in waiting.

"Rue Taitbout, 46," he directed.

But when he reached there it was to learn that his messages had been dispatched and that no power on earth could recall them.

II

CONSUMED with eager concern, Grey had himself driven to the office of the *Herald*. He was perturbed, distraught, and nervously apprehensive.

"Under a cloud," he repeated, thoughtfully; "under a cloud. That may mean anything—murder, arson, theft, elopement. I'm a fugitive from justice, I suppose. That much Frothingham made very clear when he urged my stopping those cables." And then his mood changed, and he argued that he was unnecessarily agitated. It could not be so bad. In his senses or out of them he would never, he felt sure, have committed a crime—some indiscretion, possibly, but not a crime.

When at length the file of the newspaper was before him and he was turning the pages, he noted that his fingers were unsteady and that perspiration was oozing from every pore. Carefully he scanned each headline, running down column after column with keen scrutiny. Ten minutes passed and he had reached nearly the middle of the month without finding so much as a line of what he sought. Much of the matter, however, was familiar, from which he argued that the date of revelation must be farther on. Each leaf of the book of days he turned now with dread expectation. He had been standing, the file on a table at arm's length, but suddenly he sat down, stunned by the message of the types that faced him:

"CAREY GREY AN EMBEZZLER—WELL-KNOWN WALL STREET BROKER HYPOTHECATES FIRM'S SECURITIES AND DISAPPEARS—UPWARDS OF A HUNDRED THOUSAND DOLLARS GONE."

His heart was pounding very hard and his head was bursting.

"It's a lie," he muttered, inaudibly, "an outrageous, despicable lie. It's impossible. It's preposterous. Embezzle from my own firm? It's ridiculous."

He leaned forward and pulled the file of papers down until one end rested in his lap, and then he read hastily, but with the scrupulous heed of absolute concentration, every word of the two columns that told with minute detail the story of his defalcation and flight.

"Carey Grey, of the firm of Mallory & Grey, stockbrokers, with offices in the Mills Building," began the account, "has been missing for a week and securities to the value of $110,000, it was discovered yesterday, have disappeared from the firm's safe deposit vault. Most of the securities, including first mortgage bonds of the Chicago & Northwestern Railroad Company, to the amount of $40,000, and Brooklyn Rapid Transit 5s, worth $40,000 more, Grey hypothecated, personally, with the Shoe and Leather Bank on the day prior to his flight.

"The news of the defalcation caused a sensation in the Street and in society as well. Carey Grey was one of the most popular members of the Stock Exchange and his character had always been regarded as beyond reproach. A member of an old New York family—his mother was a Livingstone—his social position was of the best. He occupied bachelor apartments in the Dunscombe, on Sixty-sixth street, near Madison avenue, and his name appears on the membership lists of the Union, Knickerbocker, and other clubs.

"Mr. Mallory, his partner, said yesterday: 'Mr. Grey was at his desk last Wednesday when I reached the office, and he was there when I went away at half-past three. There was nothing unusual in his manner. He discussed with me several matters of business and spoke of a certain directors' meeting that he should attend the next day. I have not seen or heard from him since. When he did not appear on Thursday I feared he was ill and telephoned to his rooms, but the answer came that he was not in. The whole business is to me inexplicable. I have known Carey Grey from childhood, and I would have been willing to swear that there was not a dishonest bone in his body. But the evidence against him is simply indisputable. The loss struck us at an especially bad time, but we shall pull through all right.'

"Inspector McClusky admitted that he was all at sea concerning Grey's whereabouts. The case was not reported to him for a week—not until the securities were missed—and so it was quite possible the absconder had left the country; nevertheless he was doing all in his power to locate him.

"At Grey's apartments yesterday Franz Lutz, his valet, was preparing to seek employment elsewhere.

"'Mr. Grey,' he said, 'slept here last Wednesday night. He rose about eight o'clock Thursday morning, saying he had an urgent business appointment at the Waldorf-Astoria at ten sharp. He went away in a cab, and I have not seen him since.'

"Grey's mother, who lives with her sister, Mrs. Hermann Valkenburgh, in Washington Square, North, has been prostrated by the revelations of the past twenty-four hours, and is under the care of her physician, Dr. Elbridge Bond.

"A rumour that Grey was engaged to be married to Miss Hope Van Tuyl, daughter of Nicholas Van Tuyl, president of the Consolidated Mortgage Company, was current yesterday. Miss Van Tuyl when seen last night denied the report."

There was more of it, much more, all of which Grey read with deep and astonished interest; but it was merely repetition and speculation. When he finished the two columns he turned to the paper of the day following, and found a column there. As Frothingham had told him, the newspapers had kept up the sensation for weeks, and the *Herald* was as energetic as any. At length came a report that a man answering his description had jumped overboard from a steamer in the Gulf of Mexico and had been drowned before assistance could reach him. There was nothing in his effects to give a hint as to his identity, but the world, with one accord, apparently, had accepted the suggestion that it was the missing Grey, and then the subject was dropped.

He ran through the files for another month, but other matters of more immediate interest had crowded the Grey affair out of the public thought.

He returned the papers to the clerk who had provided them, and went out onto the Avenue de l'Opéra, horrified and perplexed. He was a felon, hiding from the law. And yet never, so far as he could remember, had he harboured a dishonest impulse. He was disguised to escape detection, and the disguise when he had discovered it had been, and still was, more mystifying to himself than it could possibly be to others. Then he began to wonder what his cables would bring forth. He would be arrested, of course, and tried, and in all probability found guilty. The evidence against him as set forth in the newspaper account was not merely strong—it was irrefutable. Against the testimony of Mallory and of the bank officials what could he offer in refutation? To fancy any court or jury would put faith in his asseveration that he was unconscious when the act was committed was to count on the impossible. Nevertheless it was clearly his duty now to return at once to America and do all in his power to make reparation. And then it occurred to him that in spite of his alleged embezzlement he was, apparently, practically without funds. If he had taken the money, as charged, it must, of course, be somewhere, but of its location he had not the faintest idea. That he had disposed of a hundred or even eighty thousand dollars in five months was in the highest degree improbable.

At the corner of the Rue de la Paix is the office of Thomas Cook & Sons, and Grey entered and inquired as to the sailing of transatlantic liners. The *Celtic*, he learned, was to sail the next day from Liverpool, but he could make better time probably, the clerk told him, by taking the *Deutschland* from Boulogne, or the *Kaiser Wilhelm der Grosse* from Cherbourg, on Saturday. The tide of travel was all the other way at this season and he would have no difficulty in securing a stateroom, even at the last minute.

Resuming his stroll he had very nearly reached his hotel when a young man, pale and evidently much agitated, halted before him, and raising his hat, deferentially, said:

"A thousand pardons, Herr Arndt, but I beg you to make haste. Herr Schlippenbach—he is dying."

He spoke in German, and Grey noted that in feature and manner he was Teutonic. For an instant the American imagined the youth had addressed him by mistake, but he had sufficient presence of mind to give no sign. A second later he was reassured.

"I went to your room, Herr Arndt, as usual at four-thirty, but you were gone out, and the *portier* told me you left no message."

Grey hesitated over a reply. He realized that he was on the verge of a discovery. It was very evident now that he was not alone in Paris—that he had acquaintances, at least; probably companions; and that one of them was dying. In order to learn more he must give no indication of the change that had been wrought in him in the last few hours.

"Dying!" he exclaimed, in a tone of surprise; "I had no idea it was so serious."

His German was excellent. In his early youth he had spent two years at Göttingen, and had lived for one winter with a German family in Vienna.

"Yes," went on the young man, excitedly, "the Herr Doctor says it is a matter now of hours only, perhaps minutes. They have sent for a priest. Herr Schlippenbach—poor old Herr Schlippenbach—he is quite unconscious."

"He can recognise no one?"

"No, Herr Arndt, he just lies staring at the ceiling, and breathing very hard and loud. Oh, it is so pitiful! And the Fräulein, she is sobbing, sobbing, sobbing all the time."

Herr Arndt. So that is the name he is known by here in Paris, at the Hôtel Grammont, by those he has met—those he has travelled with, perhaps! And there is a Fräulein in the party! Herr Schlippenbach's daughter, probably. A hundred questions crowded for utterance, but he held them back.

"It was the Fräulein who sent for the priest, I suppose?" he ventured.

"Yes, Herr Arndt; she and Herr Captain Lindenwald. When Herr Schlippenbach dies Fräulein von Altdorf will have a great fortune; yes?"

"Surely," Grey hazarded. Then the girl was not the old German's daughter, after all, though she was to inherit his property. The affair was growing a trifle complicated.

"And Herr Captain Lindenwald—will he, do you think, Herr Arndt, marry the Fräulein?"

Grey was silent. If this fellow was a servant he was evidently forgetting his place, and it was well to remind him of it.

"How odd it is I never can remember your name!" he said, at length, ignoring the question and scowling a little.

"Johann, Herr Arndt."

"Yes, yes, to be sure. How stupid!"

And then they turned in at the broad marble entrance of the hotel.

III

THE room into which Johann conducted Grey was on the second floor, its windows overlooking the court. With the glare of the boulevards still in their eyes, the gloom of the darkened chamber was for a moment almost impenetrable. Grey was conscious of the presence of several persons, but they appeared more like shadows than realities, their outlines alone distinguishable. The room was very quiet, save for the sound of the laboured breathing which Johann had mentioned, and which came from a bed in an alcove to the left of the entrance. Grey stood hesitant just inside the doorway, while his vision grew accustomed to the semi-darkness; and Johann, hat in hand, stood behind him.

Presently from out of the dusk a figure approached, tiptoeing across the floor.

"He is dying!"

The words were whispered in German. The speaker, Grey observed, was of medium height, but broad of shoulder and of erect military bearing. The ends of his moustache were trained upward after the fashion affected by the German Emperor.

Grey nodded his head in token that he understood.

"Dr. Zagaie is here. He has just administered nitro-glycerine and tincture of aconite. We are hoping that he may regain consciousness."

Objects were now becoming more clearly defined. Grey could see the bed now, though its occupant was hidden by the bulky form of the physician, who had his fingers on the dying man's pulse, and by the black-clad, slender figure of a woman who was pressing a handkerchief to her eyes. At the foot of the bed stood a white-capped and white-cuffed nurse.

"Let us hope," Grey responded.

The situation was most trying. He was with those who, it was apparent, knew him extremely well, and yet were to him utter strangers. He was almost afraid to speak lest he betray himself, and if the necessity for learning something concerning his associates and associations had not been so urgently important he would have retreated without waiting further developments. He was nervously a-tremble, his fingers were twitching involuntarily and alternately waves of hot and cold bathed him from head to heel. The atmosphere of the room stifled him; the stertorous breathing of the invalid oppressed him, the gloom and the whispers and the soft tread of the persons present drove him frantic. He was seized with an almost uncontrollable impulse to shout, to rush about, to pull back the curtains and let in some daylight. He gripped his hat until the brim cracked in his hand, the sound cutting the silence discordantly.

"Sit down, Herr Arndt. We are expecting the Reverend Father. I sent Lutz for him half an hour ago."

Lutz! Had the dusk been less deep the surprise that came over Grey's features must have been observed. Lutz! Could it be possible that his valet was here in Paris with him, he asked himself. And instantly he negatived the answer. Such a supposition was beyond reason. He had misunderstood, or it was another Lutz. The name was not uncommon.

He placed his hat on a table and took a chair near a window, from which he could look into the court below. The man who had addressed him joined the group at the bedside. Johann quietly opened the door and went out, closing it as quietly behind him. The silence became painful. The inhalations and exhalations of the patient grew less strident. The sobs of the Fraülein, which had at intervals punctured the stillness, were suppressed.

Then, of a sudden, there was a commotion about the bed. The dying man, who for hours had been gazing fixedly at the ceiling, turned his eyes upon his watchers and moved his head feebly. The doctor beckoned the nurse.

"Raise his head and shoulders a trifle. Quick, another pillow!"

Promptly and deftly the nurse obeyed.

"The stimulants are acting," murmured the Herr Captain to the Fraülein: "he has responded, but it will be but temporary."

She wiped her eyes with her wet handkerchief, but said nothing. The invalid's gaze passed each of the four in turn. Then his lips moved, and the doctor, bending down, placed his ear close to his mouth.

"Monsieur Arndt," the physician said, in a low tone, as he straightened himself, "it is Monsieur Arndt that he wants."

The other three turned towards Grey. Captain Lindenwald raised his hand with a beckoning gesture.

"He wants you," he whispered; and as the American approached the bed they made way for him. It was a face very thin and drawn that met Grey's view. Very sallow, too, and parchment-like; the nose long and peaked, and the under lip, where it showed above the snow-white beard, darkly purple. A great shock of hair vied with the pillows in whiteness. In the tired eyes was a look of recognition.

"Lean over," said Dr. Zagaie; "he wishes to speak to you. His voice is very weak."

A sensation of repulsion had swept over Grey at sight of the old man, and now, to bring his face close to that of the invalid upon whom death had already set its mark was sickeningly repugnant. But with an effort of will he bent his head. A withered, wrinkled hand gripped his wrist and for the hundredth part of a second he recoiled. The voice that breathed into his ear was little more than a sigh, and he strained to gather the words.

"Take it," he heard; "it is yours. The key——"

And then the utterances sank so low as to be unintelligible. That the old man had spoken in English was a circumstance over which Grey marvelled quite as much as he did over the ambiguous command. He stood erect again and would have stepped back, but the grip of the sufferer was still upon his arm. Then, from the glazing eyes came an appeal that was unmistakable, and again Grey bent his ear.

"The throne," breathed the voice feebly; "it is yours. Take it!" This much the listener heard quite clearly, mentally commenting that the speaker was delirious. But from the sentences that followed he could only glean a word here and there. "Key" was mentioned again, and "box," and he thought he heard "proofs," and something that sounded like "Gare du Nord."

At length the fingers on his wrist relaxed and the eyes of Herr Schlippenbach closed. Instantly and with professional celerity Dr. Zagaie plunged the needle of a hypodermic syringe into the fainting man's arm. Simultaneously there was a gentle tap on the door, and without waiting to be bidden a florid-faced priest entered, carrying a small black leather case.

Grey resumed his place by the window, his brain teeming with problems so enigmatical as to defy even theoretical solution. The dying man was delirious, of course, he argued; therefore his words were unworthy of consideration. And yet, he answered himself, he had made a supreme effort to convey a message and he had chosen to phrase it in not his own tongue but his listener's, to make sure that it would be understood. He felt like a man in a maze. At every turn there was some new surprise; and he was going on and on, getting farther and farther into the tangle, without as yet seeing any chance of extricating himself.

Meanwhile, unnoticed by him, preparations for the Sacrament of Extreme Unction were being hurriedly made. The priest had donned his alb and stole and poured from a cruet the holy oil. The next minute the voice of the cleric, clear and distinct, cleaving the hush of the room, startled Grey from his meditation. The droning of the Latin ritual, solemn and awesome, struck a new chord in his emotional being. He got to his feet and stood with clasped hands and bowed head. Now the priest was anointing the dying man's eyes. With oily thumb he made the sign of the cross and recited the words: "Through this holy unction, and His most blessed mercy, may the Lord pardon thee whatever sins thou hast committed by thy sight, Amen." And then his ears, his nose, his mouth, his hands, his feet were each in turn anointed with the same form of supplication.

The ceremony concluded, Dr. Zagaie again stepped forward, taking the place vacated by the priest. As he did so Herr Schlippenbach, who had been breathing softly, peacefully, with closed lids, opened his eyes wide with a look of sudden horror. There was a quick, convulsive movement that stirred the coverlet, a long deep-drawn sigh, and the aged man lay motionless.

Fraülein von Altdorf turned away, grief-stricken and horrified, from the spectacle of death, and Grey for the first time saw her face. It was more than pretty, he thought, with its big, sad blue eyes and its full, red-lipped mouth all a-quiver with emotion. And her hair, which shone even in the dusk of that darkened apartment with a lustre of its own imparting, was very abundant and very beautiful. He realised that she was coming towards him and he took a step forward to meet her. She raised her arms and stretched out her hands gropingly until they rested on his shoulders, and instinctively he knew that she had grown suddenly faint. He clasped her swaying figure about the waist and supported her to a couch.

"Dr. Zagaie," he called, impatiently, "Mlle. von Altdorf requires a restorative."

Captain Lindenwald, who had been speaking to the nurse, turned solicitously at the words.

"My dear," he cried, kneeling beside the prostrate girl, "my dear, let me get you some wine; the strain has been too much for you."

But the Fräulein motioned him away.

"I shall be quite myself presently," she said.

Nevertheless Dr. Zagaie insisted on her taking a sedative.

After a little Grey withdrew, and not without some difficulty found his apartment, which was on the same floor, but in another part of the hotel. In his absence his room had been put in order, and there now lay upon the table a blue envelope, addressed in a distinctly English hand to "M. Max Arndt." Though it was undoubtedly meant for him it was with rather a sense of impropriety that he took it up and tore off the end. Revelation after revelation had followed one another so rapidly that afternoon that he was growing callous to discovery, and when he read—

MY DEAR MAX:

I shall be unable to dine with you tonight as I promised, but will meet you later in the Café Américain if you can arrange it—say between eleven and midnight. JACK.

—it was with scarcely a tremour of surprise. Indeed there was something in the tone of the scrawl—something, perhaps, in the penmanship, that gave him a sense of reassurance. The dying Herr Schlippenbach had affected him oddly. Nearness to him had produced a sort of emotional nausea, and for some reason which he could not explain he had experienced a violent antipathy to Captain Lindenwald. He realized that, surrounding the little company of which he had so strangely found himself one, there was a mystery which baffled his understanding. Then the last words of the old German recurred to him, and again he pondered as to whether they bore any significance or were merely the murmurings of dementia. As the clock on the mantel-shelf chimed seven, a knock sounded on the door, and in answer to his "Entrez!" Johann entered.

"Will Herr Arndt dress for dinner?" he asked. "Herr Captain Lindenwald is not dressing, and thought perhaps Herr Arndt would dine with him in the *salle à manger*. Fräulein von Altdorf is indisposed, and is having some tea and toast in her room."

"No, Johann," Grey replied, after a moment's consideration, "I won't dress. Give my compliments to the Herr Captain, and say that I'm feeling a bit seedy and will dine here alone, if he will be so good as to excuse me."

Johann bowed and was about to go, but stopped with his hand on the doorknob.

"Will Herr Arndt order his dinner now?" he queried; and Grey named the dishes.

His appetite, he all at once discovered, was excellent, and when the table had been spread and the courses followed one another in leisurely succession and with admirable service, he found himself eating with the relish that betokens good digestion. It seemed, too, when he had finished and lighted a cigarette that he could think more calmly and coherently. The windows of his room opened upon a narrow balcony, and placing a chair he stepped out and sat there meditative above the changeful tide of the boulevard which flowed unceasingly below.

He was no longer exercised over the possible effect of his cables, for he reflected that Carey Grey, so far as all Paris save one man knew, was still dead. A message or a messenger to the Hôtel Grammont would find no such person. His changed appearance, his changed name, and his changed associates were a disguise that must prove quite impenetrable. He would therefore have ample time, unhampered by either enemies or friends, to delve into the perplexing riddle that confronted him. It would be policy, he argued, to delay his return to America until he could trace his movements abroad. The difficulties that he must encounter he did not pretend to belittle. When he strove to lay out a plan of action he was balked at the very outset. To ask questions was to betray himself, and yet it must be a very long and tedious, not to say perilous, procedure to attempt to drift blindly with the current without either chart or compass to warn him of rocks and shoals.

The twilight deepened into night, and as the stars sparkled into the darkening canopy above the electric lights flashed into a brighter brilliancy along the boulevard below. Grey's cigarette had been tossed away, and he sat listlessly watching the vari-coloured lamps of the cabs as they passed to and fro—now a green, now a red, now a yellow. He had moved his chair to the space of balcony between the windows to escape an annoying draft, and from where he sat he could neither see into his room nor be seen from it. The scratching of a match inside, however, was plainly audible. Someone evidently was lighting his candles. And then the sound of voices came to him, and he pricked his ears.

"It is indeed a catastrophe," he heard. The speaker was Johann. The accent was unmistakable.

"You have no idea. It is worse, a thousand times worse than you know——"

Grey, with difficulty, choked back an exclamation.

"Lutz!" he muttered to himself, in astonishment. "By all that's good! Lutz! Here in Paris, and with me."

"Yes," the valet continued, "Herr Schlippenbach was necessary to Herr Arndt. Without Herr Schlippenbach, Herr Arndt is another man. He is mad, Johann, and filled with wild notions. He does not know his own people. He fancies he is someone else. Herr Schlippenbach was his balance wheel."

"So!" murmured Johann. "So!"

"I have a great fear we shall never get him to Kürschdorf at all."

"But the Herr Captain?"

"Oh, yes, the Herr Captain will do his best, I am sure," Lutz assented; "but it will be a mad Prince, and not a sane one, he will have on his hands."

The comment that Johann made was not distinguishable. They were going towards the door, which Grey next heard open and then close sharply, forced by the draft from the window.

IV

IT lacked but a few minutes of midnight when Grey entered the smoke-clouded air of the Café Américain. The great room was crowded and the babel of voices and the clatter of glass and china were wellnigh deafening. He stood for a moment near the door, looking about through half-closed lids like one near-sighted. A dark, languorous-eyed woman, gorgeous in scarlet silk and lace, smiled and beckoned him, but he paid no heed. He forced his way between the closely aligned tables to the centre of the room, glancing from right to left as he proceeded. His imagination had pictured his correspondent as a youngish, fair man, but he realised that his imagination was not to be relied on. He must depend on being seen and recognised, since recognition on his part was impossible. A waiter brushed against him, spattering him with beer from jostled glasses. A pretty brunette in a white gown and a great rose-trimmed hat of coarse straw seized his hand and pressed it suggestively as she passed him on her way to the door. And then, over near the mirrored wall to the right, he saw a man standing, his arm raised to attract attention, a smile on his honest, sun-browned face; and he knew it was "Jack." He was tall and spare, all muscle and sinew, and his hair was brightly red, as also was his rather close-cropped moustache.

"Gad, man," he exclaimed, as Grey came to him, "I fancied you weren't to be here."

He spoke with the pleasant brogue of the North of Ireland, and his voice and manner were as confidence-inspiring as had been his note.

Grey smiled, with something of embarrassment in his eyes. The very frankness of the other man was disconcerting. It had been comparatively easy to hide his simulation from the others, but now it was different. This big, hearty fellow was not only all honesty himself, but he inspired honesty—he demanded it.

"To tell the truth," the American replied, feeling that a confession was about to be wrung from him, "I've had a rather wretched day."

Jack looked at him keenly, his lips pressed tight in cogitation, as Grey ordered a *grenadine*.

"What's the trouble, old chap?" he asked presently, throwing back his head and sending an inverted cone of cigarette smoke ceilingward. "Tell me about it; you don't look well; you are pale and—by Jove! What's the matter with your voice? You don't speak like yourself. If I didn't see you sitting there I'd fancy it was another man who spoke."

"Would you, really?" Grey asked. The information, seeing that it was necessary for him to keep up his masquerade for awhile, was disconcerting.

"Really, you have quite lost something—or perhaps I should say you have gained something. Your tone now has some colour, some modulation. Yesterday you spoke like— you'll pardon me, won't you?—you spoke like an automaton."

"Would you mind giving me an imitation?" Grey laughed. "Oh, yes, I am serious. I want to hear you. After awhile I'll tell you why."

"Since it is your pleasure, my dear Max," Jack replied in an even drone at low pitch, "I am only too delighted to do as I am bidden. There you are! That's not exaggerated the least bit, either."

"Thank you," Grey said; and then he sat for a full minute in silence. He was impelled to make a clean breast of the whole astounding affair to this man and ask his aid. Though he was unacquainted even with his name he felt he could trust him. In this sudden and inexplicable faith his aversion for Herr Schlippenbach and Captain Lindenwald found its antithesis. He nevertheless appreciated the importance of extreme caution, and his judgment warred for the moment with his impulse. Finally a truce was signed.

"Was yesterday's tone an affectation or is today's?" asked the Irishman jocularly.

Grey took a sip at the pink contents of his glass.

"Neither," he answered, seriously; "yesterday I was asleep; today I am awake."

"Tut, tut, man! Don't talk in riddles," the other protested. "You were no more asleep last night at Maxim's than you are this minute. By the way, did you see your friend Sarema as you came in? She was sitting quite near the door a little while ago."

"Sarema?"

"To be sure. Come, come, my lad, has your mood changed as well as your tone and voice? You certainly remember the odalisque from the Folies Bergères."

Grey's eyes showed that his astonishment was unfeigned.

"Oh, but this is marvellous," cried Jack, leaning forward, his arms on the table. "You weren't drunk, man. You—you certainly weren't asleep."

"What is your name?" Grey asked, suddenly.

"Fancy!" exclaimed the Irishman. "Have you forgotten that, too? John James O'Hara, lieutenant in His Majesty's Second Dragoon Guards, of Kirwan Lodge, Drumsna, County Leitrim, at your service, sir. And you'll be telling me next, I suppose, that you don't remember meeting me in the smoke-room of the *Lucania* the first day out of New York, and that over two months ago."

"As God is my judge," Grey answered, solemnly, "I have no recollection of ever seeing you before tonight."

O'Hara's muscles stiffened and then relaxed. There was no incredulity in his face, only wonder.

"And have you forgotten your own name, too?" he queried, after a moment.

"I never knew the name I am called by until today."

"Gad, man, you're crazy," the Irishman commented, lighting a fresh cigarette. "You've got me all of a tangle. I'm damned if you're not uncanny. And your name is not Max Arndt at all, then?"

"No."

"And Herr Schlippenbach. He is not your uncle?"

"God forbid!"

"And the Fräulein von Altdorf is not your sister's daughter, I suppose?"

"I never had a sister."

The dragoon guard threw up his hands.

"Then, if it's all the same to you," he continued, "and not revealing any State secrets, would you be so good as to tell me who you are? Introduce yourself to me. For it seems that though we've been together the better part of two months we're still strangers."

Grey made a rapid but careful survey of his neighbours. Under the circumstances it might not be well to speak his own name where it could be overheard. He took another drink of his *grenadine* before replying.

"After all," he said, "this is hardly the place for confidences. What do you say to walking over to my hotel? We can have privacy there."

And Lieutenant O'Hara readily consented.

At the door of the Hôtel Grammont a courier was in excited dispute with the *portier*.

"But he will be here tomorrow, perhaps. Is it not so?"

"I cannot say. There is no Monsieur Grey here now, of a certainty."

"You are sure? You are most sure?"

"Is it not that I have said it twenty—thirty—a hundred times?" insisted the *portier*. "And you are not the only one who has asked. There have been three others here, including an agent of police. Ah, Monsieur Grey! He had better stay away, perhaps."

When at length the room of the American was reached and the door locked on the inside, Grey turned to his friend.

"Did you overhear the conversation below?" he asked.

"I caught snatches of it. A wire for someone, wasn't it?"

"Yes; for me."

"For you?" O'Hara stared. "Then why in God's name didn't you take it?"

"I couldn't afford to, and yet I'd give a good deal to know its message."

"But it was for a person named Grey, I thought. You are Grey, then?"

"Yes."

"And the police officer! He was looking for—you?"

"For me," Grey confessed. "Now you can understand why I didn't care to talk in the café."

O'Hara dropped into a chair.

"This is very interesting," he said, and his blue eyes twinkled.

Grey, his hands in his trousers' pockets, was standing before the chimney-piece. His expression was very grave.

"I suppose," he began, "that you think me rather a blackguard. Appearances so far are against me, aren't they? By my own admission I'm here under an assumed name trying to evade the minions of the law, who are hot-foot on my trail. Everything you thought you knew about me I have informed you is false. Therefore you are not likely to be predisposed in my favour. Consequently the story I'm going to tell you now you'll probably not believe. I'm free to admit that if the situation were reversed I wouldn't believe you; and yet—I—well, I wouldn't have taken you into my confidence if it were not that I'm sure you're a gentleman—an honest, high-principled, Irish gentleman who loves right and is willing to fight for it."

O'Hara smiled encouragingly.

"Drive ahead, my boy," he urged; "the jury is absolutely unprejudiced."

Then Grey plunged into a detailed narrative of that surprising day. He told of his strange awakening and parenthetically gave his hearer an idea of his position at home and a glimpse of his previous life. He rehearsed his conversation with Frothingham; he repeated word for word the cables he had sent to New York; he summarized the articles he had read in the *Herald*; he described the passing of Herr Schlippenbach and recited his death-bed communication, and finally he gave, as nearly as he could remember it, the conversation between Lutz and Johann.

O'Hara listened with rapt interest, interrupting him now and then with a question, at times smiling understandingly and at others scowling at what he regarded as evidence of importance against the little group by which Grey was surrounded. At the conclusion of the recital he sprang up and impulsively grasped the American's hand.

"You'll come out on top yet, boy," he cried, "and it's John James O'Hara that'll help to put you there. I've heard of such cases as this before. They've been drugging you, lad, that's as plain as the nose on my face, and your dear uncle, Herr Schlippenbach, do you mind, has been the chief drugger. It was because he was too ill to do his work that the effects wore off. Now that he's gone they're worried to death over you. Sure, you're not so blind that you can't see that yourself."

"But I don't understand——"

"Of course you don't. Neither do I. There's a lot we have got to find out. But two heads are better than one; and you just put a big bundle of trust in mine."

He was excited and his brogue, Grey thought, was delightful.

"What do you suggest?"

"In the first place it is probably best that I tell you what little I know. Your memory, up until this afternoon, is a blank. Well, then, I'll give you the benefit of mine."

O'Hara lighted another cigarette and, taking a deep inhalation, started pacing the floor, his head bent thoughtfully forward.

"As I said," he began, "we met in the smoke-room of the *Lucania* on the afternoon of Saturday, the seventh of April. You told me your name was Max Arndt, that you were born in Kürschdorf, the capital of Budavia, where your uncle, Herr Schlippenbach, whom you accompanied, had at one time been tutor in the royal family. You had spent your life, however, in the United States, had been engaged in the importation of German wines, I think you said, in New York, and were now on your way back to your native town, where, by the death of a relation, you had recently come into large estates. The man Lutz was with you, but he appeared to be old Schlippenbach's valet rather than yours. On reaching Liverpool you were met by Captain Lindenwald, who is of the royal household of the Kingdom of Budavia, and by the fellow Johann. After about a week in London your party was joined by Miss von Altdorf, who had been at school somewhere in Kent. You told me she was your sister's child, an orphan, and that your uncle and yourself supported her."

"Great God!" exclaimed Grey, amazedly, "and did I seem sane—rational?"

"Perfectly," O'Hara answered; "you were the character to the smallest detail. Your voice was the only peculiar thing about you. You spoke like a deaf man, with practically no inflection."

"Did you talk to Schlippenbach?"

"Oh, yes; frequently. He was really very clever. He had a wonderful fund of general knowledge. There was scarcely a subject with which he was not familiar. But his specialty was phrenology. He told me that in his youth he had known Dr. Spurzheim, the pupil of Dr. Franz Gall, the founder of the science, that he had studied under him and gone very deeply into the matter. He was a chemist, too, and from something he let drop one day I got the impression that he had experimented considerably with anæsthetics, narcotics, and that sort of thing."

"And to some purpose, apparently," put in Grey. "But his object, O'Hara? What in heaven's name could have been his object? I never knew him—never saw him to my recollection until he was dying."

"Ah, lad, we haven't got that far yet, but we'll know before we're through."

And then he went on with his story. He was with the quartet a great deal in London, he said. He showed them about, and they were all very appreciative. They stopped there until the middle of May and then they moved on to Paris. Without any intention of prying into their affairs he had observed that Herr Schlippenbach and Captain Lindenwald had a good deal of correspondence with parties in Kürschdorf.

"And what was my attitude towards them all?" Grey inquired. "Was I very sociable or was I reserved?"

"You were rather dignified," O'Hara answered; "and now I come to think of it, they treated you with considerable deference, though they endeavoured to dissemble it whenever I was about. Miss von Altdorf seemed quite fond of you, old chap, and it was amusing to note how Captain Lindenwald insisted on making love to her at every opportunity, only to be gently, but firmly, repulsed. As for that young woman I found her most charming,—and you did too, apparently. Of course, as she was your niece, you could take her to dine tête-à-tête and to places of amusement unchaperoned, and you did very frequently, much to Lindenwald's annoyance. Whatever the plot is, Grey, I feel satisfied that she is not in it."

"And now what do you advise?"

"For the present at least to give no sign that you suspect anything. You are well enough posted now, my boy, to go straight ahead. Give them enough rope and they'll hang themselves as sure as your name's Grey and mine's O'Hara. Assume the tone I told you of, and they'll never suspect. They may be surprised, but they'll be happy and they'll be unwary. Never take the initiative yourself. Leave it all to Lindenwald."

"But what will they make out of it?" Grey urged, curiously. "Surely you have formed some theory?"

"Yes, I have a theory," O'Hara responded, "but it is probably just as well for me to keep it to myself for a while."

"What do you think this talk about 'thrones' and 'mad princes' means?"

"That is for us to find out. And unless I am more of a fool than I think, it will very shortly develop. In the meantime you are anxious about the answers to your cables, aren't you? Since they are addressed to Grey, you can't accept them, that's clear. But you shall know what is in them just the same. I'll undertake that for you."

"But——"

"Never mind, lad; leave it to me."

"And the box with proofs that Schlippenbach spoke of? That is important."

"To be sure. It is at the Gare du Nord in his name or yours, eh? I'll get it for you. But the key?"

Suddenly Grey remembered.

"There is a key in a wallet I found. Possibly that is it."

"Possibly."

And the thought of the wallet reminded him that a fifty-franc note and some change was all the money he had in his possession.

"I'm a little short of funds," he said. "Do you happen to know how or where I have been in the habit of getting money when I needed it?"

O'Hara laughed.

"The whole thing is so absurd," he explained, "as well as serious. Fancy your not knowing what you have done every few days since you landed! Johann has your letter of credit and gets you whatever you desire. All that is necessary is for you to sign your name."

When O'Hara had gone Grey sat for a long time brooding over his extraordinary experience. His head was still aching, throbbingly, and his nerves were still a-tingle. Whatever treatment he had been subjected to its effects had not yet been entirely eliminated. He undressed, got into his pyjamas and went to bed; but sleep was coy and not to be won by wooing. He heard the clock strike two and three and four, and he saw the first gray sign of dawn between his curtains before he fell into a restless, troubled, unrefreshing slumber.

V

MR. HERBERT FROTHINGHAM had that evening been one of a dinner party of six at Armenonville. He had sat between Miss Hope Van Tuyl and Lady Constance Vincent, and across a plateau of primrose-coloured orchids the charming Mrs. Dickie Venable had at intervals favoured him with fleeting smiles. Nicholas Van Tuyl, sleek and ruddy, was at the left of Lady Constance, who had for her vis-à-vis Sinclair Edson, a tall, young, sallow-faced secretary from the United States Embassy.

"I hope you haven't failed to observe the notabilities," this latter-named gentleman was saying as he daintily dissected his *carpe au buerre noir*; "there are quite a number here this evening." His pose as mentor was apt to grow annoying at times, but the Van Tuyls had been in Paris only two days, and father and daughter were alike interested.

"Oh, do show me that East Indian prince or whatever he is," cried Hope enthusiastically, her great dark eyes brilliant; "I've heard so much of him. Is he here?"

"The Maharajah of Kahlapore? Yes, he must be here, surely. I never come nowadays but he is."

He turned his head and craned his neck in an effort to locate the Hindu potentate. The piazza of the pavilion was, as usual, crowded. Every table was occupied—and the throng was the acme of cosmopolitanism. Five continents were represented. It was indeed a veritable congress of nations. Monarchs, kings dethroned, and pretenders rubbed elbows. Women of the world and of the half-world brushed skirts. Dazzling toilets of delicate tints were silhouetted against coats of lustreless black. Diamonds blazed; pearls reflected the myriad lights; gems of all colours, shapes, and sizes glistened in the foreground and sparkled in remote corners.

"Ah, there he is," Edson discovered, speaking without turning his face; "there, off to the right. You can just see his white turban over the head of that Titian-haired woman in the blue gown."

The whole party stared, stretching, twisting to get a glimpse.

"Rather insignificant, isn't he?" observed Mrs. Dickie disparagingly.

"His turban accentuates his *café au lait* complexion," laughed Hope.

"But you should see him at finger-bowl time," suggested Lady Constance, who had lunched next to him and his suite that day at Paillard's. "He is most original."

"Oh, tell us," cried Hope pleadingly; "what does he do?"

"It must be seen to be appreciated," the Englishwoman replied. She was auburn-haired, generously proportioned, and rather stolid. Her tone was even more of a refusal than her words.

"I'll tell you," volunteered Edson glibly. "He has a special bowl twice the ordinary size and he plunges his whole face in it."

"Horrors!" shrieked Mrs. Dickie; "he should be arrested for attempted suicide."

"But he isn't the most interesting personage here by any means," Edson pursued, now thoroughly launched in the exercise of his *métier*, "have you noticed the sallow-faced, heavy-browed and long-moustached gentleman just three tables away, dining with the dark-bearded president of the Chamber of Deputies?"

"The man with that enormous, gorgeously jewelled star on his breast?" asked Miss Van Tuyl, leaning back and gazing over Frothingham's shoulder. "Oh, what a brutal face he has!"

"It is the Shah of Persia," announced Edson; and then he glanced about to revel in the effect of his revelation.

"He's a beast," commented Lady Constance, disgustedly, "though I believe his manners have improved somewhat since he was here last. Do you know when he was in Berlin some years ago he sat next to the Empress Augusta at a State banquet, and whenever he got anything in his mouth that was not to his taste, he just calmly removed it!"

"They say he thought nothing of putting his hands on the bare shoulders of the women he met," Edson added.

"I saw the King of the Belgians as we came in," said Mr. Van Tuyl, presently, as a waiter passed the *filet aux truffes*; "one sees him everywhere, eh?"

"Oh, yes," Edson hastened to observe; "he's as omnipresent as the poor. But did you see the woman with him? She's the very latest, you know. Was a *Quartier Latin* model six months ago and is now regarded as the most beautiful woman in Paris. *La Minette Blanche*, they call her. She has a palace on the Boulevard Malesherbes and as many retainers as a princess."

"The old scoundrel!" exclaimed Mrs. Dickie, vindictively; "I don't know which is worse, the Shah or he. He gained a reputation as a wife-beater or something, didn't he? At all events I'll bet the devil is keeping a griddle hot for him down below, and it's pretty near time he occupied it."

"How terribly spiteful!" laughed Frothingham; "His Majesty isn't a bad sort at all; a little fickle, perhaps, but with his love of beauty and his opportunities you can hardly expect domesticity. And he's done a lot of good in his way."

"Speaking of royalty, that is rather an odd condition of affairs in Budavia, by the way," suggested Nicholas Van Tuyl. "Did you see the paper this morning? The King is very ill. Can't live a fortnight; and there is a question as to the succession. It seems that the Crown Prince was kidnapped when he was five years old and nothing has ever been heard of him. They don't know whether he is alive or dead."

"Oh, how interesting!" exclaimed Mrs. Dickie, putting down her fork to listen. "And to whom does the crown go?"

"To King Frederic's nephew, Prince Hugo; as thorough a reprobate, they say, as there is in all Europe."

"Wouldn't it be funny if the Crown Prince should turn up at this juncture?" suggested Edson; and there was something significant in his tone.

"Has such a possibility been hinted at?" asked Van Tuyl.

"Well—" and Edson hesitated the briefest moment, "one can never tell." Whether intentionally or not, he gave the impression that he knew more than he cared to divulge. "I had a call today from an officer of the Budavian army. He is a member of the royal household." He said this with an air, and Frothingham muttered, "Snob!" under his breath.

"I suppose he spoke of the situation, eh?" asked Van Tuyl.

"Yes, of course, he referred to it. I met him last year in Vienna. His call was purely social."

"Is he to be in Paris long?" asked Mrs. Dickie, quickly. "Bring him to tea next Tuesday."

But Edson evaded a promise. He was listening to Frothingham, who was saying:

"You can never tell when or where or under what circumstances a lost man will reappear. After today I shall make it a rule not to believe a man is dead unless I have seen him buried."

"Why, whom on earth have you seen?" questioned Miss Van Tuyl. There was just the slightest suspicion of a tremour in her voice, and her eyes were apprehensive. The speaker, however, detected neither. He had, in fact, quite forgotten, if he had ever heard, that there had been an attachment between the man he had that day met on the *terrasse* of the Café de la Paix and the woman who sat at his side.

"Carey Grey, the absconder!"

The words struck her as a blow from a clenched fist. Her cheeks, which had been a trifle flushed, went suddenly white as the damask napery. Her jewelled fingers clutched the edge of the table. She felt that she was falling backward, that everything was receding, and she caught the table edge to save herself.

"Carey Grey!" repeated Nicholas Van Tuyl, in amazement. "Surely you must have been mistaken!"

"Not a bit of it. I talked to him."

"The devil!" exclaimed Edson and then apologised.

"You'd never know him," Frothingham went on, after emptying his champagne glass; "he has bleached his hair, and he is wearing a bleached beard, too."

"Oh, horrible!" This from Mrs. Dickie.

"Told a most remarkable story about not knowing anything for five months; brain fever or something. I must admit he was very convincing."

"I wonder if that is the man I knew?" Lady Constance broke in. "He came over with an American polo team; he was a great friend of Lord Stanniscourt's."

"Same man," said Van Tuyl, with a glint of admiration in his tone. "He was a capital polo player, and—yes, by Jove, a rattling good fellow in every way. It was a surprise to everyone when he went wrong." He had been watching his daughter with no little anxiety. Now her colour was returning and her hands were in her lap.

"Yes, to everyone," Mrs. Dickie volunteered, "the whole thing was simply astounding. He had a good business, hadn't he? What do you suppose he wanted with that money?"

"Nobody was ever able to conjecture," answered Frothingham, as he helped himself to some *caneton*.

"And he is really here in Paris?" queried Edson, twirling the long stem of a fragile wineglass between thumb and finger. "Where is he stopping?"

Hope Van Tuyl unconsciously leaned forward to catch the address.

"I don't know. I never thought to inquire."

From the violins of the tziganes glided the languorous strains of the "Valse Bleue," and instantly all other sounds dwindled. Even the clatter of knives and forks seemed gradually to cease and the babble of tongues was vague and far away. Into the girl's dark eyes came an expression of melancholy, and the corners of her red-lipped mouth drooped. The leaves of her calendar had been fluttered back a twelvemonth by the melody, and she was out under the stars with the cool breeze from the Hudson fanning her flushed cheeks. Through the open French windows of the clubhouse at her back the music was floating. Beside her, his arm girdling her waist, was the man to whom she had just promised her love and loyalty—the man whose name she would be proud to wear through all her days—Carey Grey. The ineffable joy, the blissful content of the moment were, in some mystic manner, reborn by the chords that sang and swelled and vibrated and whispered, and yet over all, mingling with the delicious, intoxicating happiness of this reincarnated experience, was an overpowering sense of loss—dire, monstrous, crushing.

"Hope, dear,"—it was her father's voice that brought her back to the present. His anxious eyes had still been upon her. "Drink your wine, girl; you aren't ill, are you? Mr. Edson has been speaking to you and I don't believe you've heard a word."

"Oh, I beg your pardon, Mr. Edson," she ejaculated, recovering herself. "I fear for the moment I was very far off. Would you mind repeating what you said?"

"I was proposing a coaching party to Versailles for Saturday, and as everybody seemed to approve I took the opportunity to ask you if you would do me the honour of occupying the box seat."

"With pleasure," she accepted, smiling bravely, though a dull, leaden pain was gripping her heart; "I think it will be simply lovely."

The sextet had come to the restaurant crowded into Mr. Edson's big touring car, and when at length the dinner was finished and the men had smoked their cigars and the moon had come up from behind the trees and floated like a silver boat in the deep blue sea of the heavens, they took their places again and went spinning at frantic speed out into the Allée de Longchamp. A quick turn to the left and in another instant the Porte Dauphine had been passed and the machine was flying smoothly down the Avenue du Bois de Boulogne with the Arc de Triomphe rising massively white in the moonlight ahead.

Frothingham found himself brought very close to Hope Van Tuyl by the exigencies of the arrangement of six goodly sized persons in a space designed for five; and he was glad that it was so. He had seen much of her during the winter season in New York, and he had come abroad chiefly because he knew that she and her father had planned to spend the early summer in Europe. She was the type of woman he admired. She was tall and athletic, fond of sports and clever at them, but not so much of an enthusiast as to be open to the charge of having unsexed herself. She was, indeed, intensely feminine. Though she could handle a coach and four as dexterously as the average masculine whip and could drive a golf ball well on to two hundred yards, her hands were as delicately white and her fingers as long and taper as those of a girl whose most strenuous exertion was the execution of a Chopin nocturne. Her hair was dark, almost black, with glinting bronze reflections in the sunlight. Her eyes were the brown of chestnuts and her eyebrows black and perfectly arched. Frothingham had dreamed night after night of her mouth—it was so red and so tenderly curved, and her lips seemed always moist.

He had noticed her preoccupation towards the close of the dinner, and he had marvelled as to the cause. It was such an unusual mood for her. Now, as they were sweeping with exhilarating speed down the long avenue, with its double row of glittering lights that flashed by in streaks—while all the rest were laughing, shouting, shrieking in the exuberance of the moment—she was still abstracted, silent.

Frothingham ventured to place a hand over one of hers, but she drew her own away instantly, as though the contact were painful. He fancied then that he had perhaps unwittingly offended her in some way, and he whispered, close to her ear:

"I hope you are not annoyed at me. Have I been guilty of any discourtesy? I am sure I——"

But it was very evident she was not listening, and he broke off in the middle of the sentence.

The Van Tuyls were stopping at the Ritz, and there Edson put them down. Frothingham, who had taken lodgings not far away, alighted too, and Nicholas Van Tuyl asked him in.

"I feel like a brandy and soda," he said, "and I want company."

Hope excused herself and went directly to her room. She was very nervous and very *distraite*. The story that Carey Grey was not only alive and in Paris, but had been ill, delirious and therefore unaccountable, disquieted and distressed her. She had loved him more than she knew until his crime and his flight, and, above all, his desertion without a word of explanation, revealed to her the fulness of her passion. Then she had battled with herself for a time; had grown philosophic and had reasoned, and eventually had gathered together the pages of her life that bore his name, had torn them out and, as she believed, destroyed them utterly. And now they were here before her, suddenly restored as a magician makes whole again the articles that he tears into bits before his auditors' eyes.

As she entered her room her maid, who had been reading near a window, arose, took up something from her dressing-table and came toward her with it in her outstretched hand.

"A telegram for m'amselle," she said. She was a very pretty French maid, and she had a very delicious French accent. She preferred to speak in English, though Miss Van Tuyl invariably answered her in French. "It came not ten minutes ago, m'amselle."

Hope walked listlessly to where an electric lamp glowed under a Dresden shade, tearing open the envelope as she went. Unfolding the inclosure, she held it in the light's glare; and then the little blue sheet dropped from her nerveless fingers, and she reeled. Had it not been for Marcelle she might have fallen; but the girl, burning with curiosity to learn the contents of the telegram—or cablegram, as it proved—had followed her mistress's every movement, and now her arm was about her waist.

"Oh, m'amselle, m'amselle," she cried in alarm; "my poor m'amselle! Is it that you hear the bad news?"

But Miss Van Tuyl made no reply. Recovering herself, she crossed the room and sat down in the chair by the window that Marcelle had just vacated. The girl stood for a moment irresolute. Then she stooped and picked up the sheet of blue paper, placing it on the table under the lamp. As she did so her quick eye took in enough to satisfy her as to its import. It was from Miss Van Tuyl's brother in New York, and it repeated a cable just received. The words made a very deep impression on Marcelle because of one of them, of which, though it was quite as much French as it was English, she did not know the meaning.

"That he is here in Paris I can understand; and that he is alive and well, oh, yes!" she iterated and reiterated to herself;

"but what is it he means by '*in-ex-pleek-able*'? 'Conditions *in-ex-pleek-able*'? Oh, I fear, I fear, that is something very terrible."

VI

THERE came a gentle tap on Grey's door; then a rap, louder and more insistent; and then repeated knocking, aggressive, commanding; and Grey, aroused suddenly from what was more stupor than sleep, sat up in bed, startled, crying:

"Come in! *Entrez! Herein!*"

The door opened and Johann entered.

"It is long after noon, Herr Arndt," he said, bowing, "and the funeral is arranged for three o'clock."

Grey rubbed his eyes and made an effort to collect his scattered senses.

"Ah, yes," he murmured, after a moment; "Herr Schlippenbach's funeral."

"It is very wet," Johann continued; "since six this morning it has been raining. I have ordered Herr Arndt's coffee. It will be here presently."

"And my tub?"

"It waits, Herr Arndt."

While Grey, in bathrobe and slippers, was sipping his *café au lait* and nibbling a *brioche*, Captain Lindenwald presented himself.

"I have arranged everything," he announced, with an air of thorough self-satisfaction; "for the present we will leave the remains here in Paris. Later we can decide whether they shall be brought on to Kürschdorf or sent back to America. I have placed all the details of the obsequies in the hands of the *Compagnie des Pompes Funèbres*. The temporary interment will be this afternoon at Père-la-Chaise. Will it be the pleasure of Herr Arndt to attend?"

Grey raised his cup to his lips and replaced it on the saucer before replying. He wished to make sure that he could rid his tone of all modulation.

"Yes," he answered, speaking with great care, "I will go." If he was to play the game it were better that he played every hand dealt to him.

After a little he asked:

"And the Fraülein von Altdorf? How is she today?"

"Oh, much better," returned the Herr Captain, his face beaming; "she is more composed, more resigned. She is a wonderful young woman, Herr Arndt; and oh, she is so beautiful!"

"Yes, she is very lovely," Grey acquiesced.

But his thoughts at the moment were not of her. Lindenwald's eulogy had set vibrant a chord of emotion, had conjured a picture, had reproduced a dream that seemed a reality. It was indeed difficult for him to reconcile the remembrance of that sleep fantasy, so vivid was it in every detail, with the knowledge that it was not a waking experience. He had sat for hours, it seemed, beside Hope Van Tuyl, gazing into the limpid depths of her sympathetic eyes, listening to the melody of her clear, full-toned voice. They were in a great garden with parterres of gay, sweet-scented flowers—roses and heliotrope and geraniums—and smooth terraces of greensward with marble nymphs and satyrs on mossy pedestals, and above them the kindly, protecting, leafy branches of an old oak. He had, he thought, just found again the girl he loved—found her after a long, long separation, and now she was close within his hungry arms and her lips were always very near his own. He was telling her some fantastic tale, like a bit culled from the Arthurian legends, of how he was a great king, and had only been away to claim his own, and now she was to be his queen and sit beside him on the throne in robes of purple and ermine and help him rule his people with justice and mercy.

Yet here he was sitting in a Paris hotel bedchamber, with a man who was almost a stranger, while the rain was pelting on the window-panes and the room was so gloomy that he could scarcely see the face of his visitor. The recollection of the dream thus contrasted filled him with a spirit of rebellion. He was beset with an impulse to reveal without further delay his true condition and let the culprits, whoever they might be, escape with their object undefined and their plunder unrestored. The craving to see and hold and talk to the woman he adored obsessed him for the moment, and he felt that all else was trivial and futile.

It was in this mood still that Jack O'Hara found him an hour later.

"I am off to America by the first steamer," he said, joyously. "It is all tommyrot following this thing up. I'm going back, tell everything as far as I know, and let the police do the rest."

The Irishman looked at him in amazement.

"What's come over you, lad?" he asked, solemnly. "Have you gone off your head or are you dreaming? Sure you're not going to back out now when we've got such a pretty little fight ahead of us, with the enemy in ambush and afraid to show their colours?"

"No, I'm not off my head," Grey replied a little less gaily. He did not like the suggested imputation of cowardice.

"Then you are dreaming, sure."

"I have been." The reply was ambiguous, but O'Hara took it that his friend had changed his mind.

"And you're not now; you're awake, wide awake, eh? And you're going to stop and rout 'em, horse, foot, and dragoon? That's right, man. What the devil put the going-home notion in your noddle? I'll wager twenty pounds it's a woman you've been thinking of."

Grey stood by the window looking out on the drenched Boulevard. O'Hara's words were an inspiration, but the face and form of Hope were still before him and her voice still echoed in his ears. The longing would not easily down.

"I've been looking after your blessed cablegrams," the Irishman went on. "There's only one there for you. I told 'em my name was Grey and opened it and read it. Then I gave it back to 'em, and explained it must be for same other Grey. I told 'em my name was Charley, and that that was addressed to Carey."

"Only one?" Grey exclaimed, in a tone of disappointment, turning. "I don't suppose Mallory will answer. What a damned blackguard he must think me! He's handed my cable over to the police, of course. I suppose extradition papers are under way by this time. But the one? What was it?"

"Here, I wrote it down so as not to forget," and O'Hara, after fumbling in his breast pocket, produced an envelope on which was written:

Overcome with joy. I never gave up hope. God bless you.—MOTHER.

Grey turned to the window again, his eyes as wet as the panes. After a little he asked:

"And that was the only one?"

"The only one."

Then Hope had not answered. She believed him guilty, of course. It would have been better to have let her, like the rest of the world, think him dead. What a trickster is the weaver of dreams! How real had seemed his vision, and yet how untrue! And he had thought of going to her as fast as the speediest ocean liner could take him. Oh, yes, he was awake now; wide, wide awake.

"I couldn't get the box at the Gare du Nord," O'Hara continued. "They'd given a brass or something for it and had no record of your name or Schlippenbach's either. You had better ask Johann about it, or Lutz."

"I will," said Grey.

A hearse had stopped before the door, and he began now putting on his gloves.

"No," he added as he buttoned the grey suèdes, "I'm not going back to America, O'Hara. Maybe I'll never go back. I'm going to Schlippenbach's funeral now, and I'm going to follow this thing to the end of the route if it takes me through hell." His face was very set and solemn, and he spoke with a determination that made O'Hara's eyes dance.

"Bravo, lad!" he cried, enthusiastically. "I still have two months' leave, and I'll go with you, hand in hand, every step of the way."

The drive to Père-la-Chaise was very long and very boresome. Captain Lindenwald was not inclined to conversation and Grey dared not attempt to lead in the direction he wished, for fear of revealing how little he knew of what had been prearranged. He gathered, however, that it had been planned to start for Budavia early in the following week and that the death of Herr Schlippenbach was not to interfere with this arrangement; but of what they were going for—of what was to follow their arrival, he could glean no hint.

On the return from the cemetery, however, an incident occurred which he regarded as significant, though it only added to his perplexity. The carriage had just crossed the Place de la République, past the great bronze statue which adorns the square, and was rolling leisurely along the Boulevard St. Martin, when Lindenwald suddenly drew back in the corner in evident trepidation, catching Grey's arm and dragging him back with him.

"For God's sake!" he whispered, excitedly. "Did you see that man?"

"What man?" Grey asked, a little annoyed. He had seen a score of men. The day was waning; the rain had ceased and there was the usual crowd that throngs the boulevards at the green hour.

Lindenwald clutched him tightly for a moment, huddled away from the window of the voiture. At this point the sidewalks are somewhat higher than the roadway and they had both been looking up at the pedestrians, more interested in the procession than in each other.

"He was standing in front of the Folies Dramatiques," Lindenwald explained, presently; "his presence here means no good."

"But who?" Grey persisted.

"It was the Baron von Einhard. You know who the Baron von Einhard is. Ah! It is very plain. In some way, in spite of all our precautions, Hugo has got word. We must now be more than careful. The Baron, my dear Herr Arndt, would not hesitate one little—one very little moment to cut your throat if he got the chance." Lindenwald shut his teeth tight, puckered his lips, and peered convincingly at Grey between half-lowered lids.

The American crushed back an exclamation of surprise. In its place he substituted an inquiry.

"What is the Baron like?" he asked, wondering whether he had seen him. The question was a risk, but he ventured.

"He is small, dark, sharp-featured. He looks more like an Italian than a Budavian, and he is vengeful. He is, too, oh, so shrewd! Six assassinations are at his door, and yet—positively, Herr Arndt, what I say is true—not one of them can be brought home to him."

"You are quite sure it was he whom you saw?"

"Oh, quite sure, of a certainty. I only trust he did not see us. But his eyes are lynx-like. If he saw us you can be assured we are even now being followed. Will it be too warm, do you think, if I lower the shade? He is not here alone, and they are on the lookout."

"As you think best," Grey replied. And Captain Lindenwald pulled down the silk covering of the window.

When at length they alighted at the Hôtel Grammont and entered the courtyard the *portier* informed the Captain that a gentleman was waiting for him in the reading-room. He went in, with Grey, who wished to look at a newspaper, closely following; and a tall, sallow-faced young man, faultlessly attired, rose and came towards them.

Grey turned aside to a table, but Lindenwald greeted the caller with no little suavity of manner.

"Ah, Monsieur Edson," he said, affably, "this is indeed an honour. You have not, I hope, been waiting long?"

"I have a favour to ask," the young diplomat replied, "and I shall take only a moment of your time, Captain. I today received advices from the State Department at Washington that there is an American stopping at this hotel whose name is Grey, though they tell me here there is no one of that name in the house. It seems he cabled to New York yesterday and gave this as his address. He is wanted for embezzlement."

Grey overheard the words and stood motionless, tense, listening eagerly. His eyes were bent over the table, but it was so dark in the room that the print of the paper before him was but a grey blur.

"And you would like me to——?" asked Lindenwald. There was no savour of agitation in his voice, and Grey wondered how much or how little he knew.

"I thought perhaps you might aid me. Fortunately I have his description. I dined in company with a man last night who has seen him. He is tall, well set-up, and has fair hair, beard and moustache."

"There are many such," replied the Captain, shrugging his shoulders.

A servant entered with a burning wax taper, and Grey stepped aside for him to light the gas over the table. As he did so he faced Edson, and the illumination lit his features.

"Ah, there," the caller whispered, a little nervously, "standing by the table behind you—there is a man of the very type. Perhaps that is he."

Captain Lindenwald turned his head.

"Ha, ha!" he laughed, clapping his hand on Edson's shoulder, "that is very droll, very. Do you remember what I told you yesterday at the Embassy?"

Edson nodded.

"Yes, yes, of course. But——"

"Well, it is he."

"He?"

"Yes, to be sure. In the strictest confidence, mind you. I would not tell you were it not that I want to assure you beyond all question that he, of all persons, cannot be suspected."

Grey smiled in spite of himself.

"That man is——"

"Sh!" warned Lindenwald his voice very low. "Yes, that man is His Royal Highness, Prince Maximilian, heir apparent to the throne of Budavia."

In spite of the low tone of the speaker Grey caught the words, and the blood went rushing to his head and set him dizzy. What monstrous lie was this? He heir apparent to the throne of Budavia! He, a descendant of plain Puritan ancestry, a republican of republicans, being posed as a royal personage! It was staggering. And this was the solution to the riddle. This was why they were going to Kürschdorf. Herr Arndt was a name assumed. The Crown Prince was travelling incognito. It was all too ridiculous. He had suspected some mad scheme from Schlippenbach's death-bed admonition and from Lutz's overheard conversation with Johann, but this comic opera dénouement was quite beyond anything he had permitted himself to fancy.

The young gentleman from the United States Embassy was evidently duly impressed. He coloured and he apologised and he looked hard at Grey to make sure that he would recognise Prince Maximilian should he again chance to see him—dining at Armenonville, for instance.

"I hope," he added, with a faint smile, "that you will not mention my stupid blunder to His Royal Highness. I should be mortified to have him know."

"Ha, ha!" laughed Lindenwald again, "he would take it as a good joke. Oh, yes, I must tell him. He will be so much amused."

Edson sidled toward the door and the Budavian officer turned to accompany him, but stopped short, his face suddenly pallid. Standing on the threshold, not five paces away, was the small, wiry, dark, sharp-featured man he had noticed on the Boulevard St. Martin.

"Good evening, Herr Captain," said the Baron von Einhard, his eyes twinkling.

Captain Lindenwald saluted in military fashion, and the Baron returned the salute as Edson brushed by him into the passage.

"You did not, I suppose, expect to see me in Paris, eh?" the newcomer observed.

"You were the last man for whom I looked, Baron," the officer rejoined. "What is the latest news from Kürschdorf?"

"You have not seen the evening papers, then?"

"No."

"His Majesty is much worse. His condition became alarming this morning, at nine o'clock. He cannot, the doctors say, live over forty-eight hours." He made the announcement with an air of pleasurable anticipation. "I should fancy, Herr Captain, that your presence might be required at the Palace. Or," and there was a world of cunning suggestion in his tone, "you have more important business here in Paris?"

"As you say, Herr Baron," Lindenwald replied, visibly uncomfortable. He was questioning whether the Baron had overheard his conversation with Edson, and if so, how much. The man's small eyes were like the eyes of a snake, beady and sinister. They compelled against one's will.

"You remain here long?" von Einhard continued, smiling insinuatingly.

"The length of my stay is undetermined."

"I trust we shall meet again," and the Baron, still smiling, bowed, turned on his heel and vanished.

Grey, who had been listening, now rejoined the Captain.

"He followed us, evidently," he ventured.

"He is a serpent," Lindenwald commented, gravely, "and one to be feared. He crawls in the grass, gives no sign and strikes with poisoned fang where and when least expected. We must be very wary—very wary, indeed, until we are quite sure he has left the city. Ah, and that is not the worst—how can we ever be sure? This is a case, Herr Arndt, where caution is more advisable than valour."

"And your advice is?" Grey queried.

"My advice is never to go out unaccompanied. Already he is setting his traps, arranging his pitfalls. You cannot conceive of his ingenuity. I am vexed because I feel myself unequal to combat his trickery. In fair fight I have no fear, but to fence with von Einhard is to be always in danger of the impalpable."

When they had separated and Grey was alone in his room, he flung himself into a comfortable chair, lighted a cigarette and gave himself up to reflection. The gravity of the affair was not to be minimized, yet he could not repress a smile as he thought of the triangular form the matter had assumed and of the complications, ramifications and cross-purposes that had developed. Personally his object was to detect and bring to justice those persons who had, for some reason not yet divulged, been using him as a cat's-paw to attain an end of which he was also ignorant. He had, of course, every reason to believe that in this plot Captain Lindenwald was a prominent factor, and as such his hand was against him. Meanwhile the machinery of international justice had been set in motion to bring about his own apprehension, extradition and punishment for a crime he had never contemplated and never willingly committed. Whether to this infraction Captain Lindenwald had been a party he had no means of knowing, but now it had turned out that another enemy was in the field—an aggressive foe seeking his life—and in this new battle Captain Lindenwald, strangely enough, was, it would seem, his staunch ally. He wondered whether any man had ever before been so harassed, so persecuted, so maligned, so humiliated through no fault of his own; and his sense of injury waxed more galling and his resentment more turbulently avid. He grew impatient of every hour's delay in the chase, restless under his enforced inaction and fretful over the tardy revelation of past events and the development of future plans.

Then the thought of the box at the Gare du Nord recurred to him, and he got up and rang for Johann. But the youth knew nothing of it.

"Lutz, perhaps," he said; "it is possible that Lutz knows. I will send him to you, Herr Arndt."

And a little later Lutz came in. His air was timid and his manner uneasy. His eyes were furtive and refused to meet his master's, and his fingers were in constant motion.

"Ah, Lutz," Grey greeted him composedly, taking great care to erase all modulation from his tone, "there is somewhere, probably among poor Herr Schlippenbach's effects, a receipt or check for a box at a railway station here in Paris—at the Gare du Nord, in fact. I wish you would see if you can find it for me."

"Yes, Herr Arndt." His gaze was on the carpet.

"Immediately, Lutz."

"Yes, Herr Arndt."

"That is all."

When he had gone Grey began pacing the floor like a madman, his fists clenched, his eyes blazing.

"Was ever guilt more apparent?" he asked himself. "It is written all over him."

And he wondered how he had controlled himself, how he had refrained from catching him by the throat and strangling a confession from him without more ado.

VII

GREY dined that evening across the Boulevard at the Maison Dorée, in company with Fräulein von Altdorf and Herr Captain Lindenwald; and, as the officer insisted that it was advisable for them to avoid as much as possible the public eye, the trio dined in a *cabinet particulier* on the second floor with windows open on the street. It was not a very gay dinner, in spite of the Herr Captain's efforts to infuse some mirth into it. Miss von Altdorf was apparently still grief-stricken over her great-uncle's sudden death, and though she strove valiantly to smile at Lindenwald's essays at wit and to respond with some animation to Grey's less jocose but cheerful observations, it was with such palpable exertion as to rather discourage her would-be entertainers.

Her youth was a surprise to the American. At first sight he had fancied her three or four-and-twenty, but he was satisfied now that she could not be more than eighteen. Her figure was distinctly girlish.

She was all in white, from her great ostrich-plumed hat of Leghorn straw to her tiny canvas bottines, because, young as she was, she entertained prejudices against conventional mourning, and exercised them. It was a question, however, whether in black or white she was more beautiful. In the death-chamber Grey had seen her sombre-robed and had pronounced her rarely lovely, and now in raiment immaculately snowy she was equally alluring. Her expression was naturally pensive and her recent sorrow had given to her big, deep-set, long-lashed blue eyes a pathos that awoke the tenderest emotions. As the American gazed at her across the table he experienced a thrill of sentiment that was undeniable, and he had but to glance at Lindenwald to see in his contemplation the same fervency of soul.

"I should like it," Grey said to her when the dinner was about over and he was burning his cognac over his coffee, "if you would take a trip with me tomorrow into the country. We will start early and have *déjeuner* at some inn, under the trees. It will do you a world of good."

Something very like a frown gathered on Lindenwald's brow, but it passed before he spoke.

"Do not forget my warning, Herr Arndt," he interjected. "It would perhaps be safer for me to accompany Fraülein von Altdorf."

"I will chance it," Grey replied, decisively. "I feel that I, too, need a little outing."

"It will be lovely, Uncle Max," the girl responded, with more animation than she had previously shown. "Let us go to Versailles. I have never been, and I have read so much about it."

"Versailles it shall be, my dear," he answered, lighting a cigarette, while Lindenwald brushed his hand across his brow to hide a scowl.

Grey's broken, unrefreshing, dreamful slumber of the night before, followed by a tiresome, distressing day, resulted early in the evening in a drowsiness that he could not shake off. For a while he dozed in a chair by an open window, but when the clock had struck eleven he arose and prepared for bed, and in a little while he was sleeping soundly behind his blue velvet curtains.

The night, however, was warm and close after the rain of the day, and, as the hours wore on, the sleeper grew restless and turned uneasily from side to side, by-and-by waking at each turning and seeking a cool spot between the sheets. At length sleep forsook him altogether, and he lay quite wide awake peering into the darkness in an effort to distinguish objects. But the night was very black and the room was enveloped in a pall of ink, save where the reflection from the street lamps spread patches of dim yellow light on wall and ceiling. The stillness, too, was oppressive. The boulevard was dead, and within doors no sound except the monotonous ticking of the clock on the mantel-shelf was audible.

He waited longingly for the clock to strike that he might know how many hours must elapse before the dawn; and as he waited, his senses alert, there broke softly on the silence the stealthy tread of feet in the passage on the other side of the wall near which he lay. No sooner had he heard the footsteps than they ceased, and the sound was succeeded by a muffled, metallic clicking from the direction of his door. With Lindenwald's warning in mind he had turned the key in the lock before retiring, and he recalled this now with a sense of satisfied security; but even as he did so he was conscious of the door being pushed slowly but creakingly ajar, and then the tread that he had heard without he heard within. He held his breath, not in affright, for he was, he realised, wonderfully composed, but lest he scare away the intruder before the object of his visit was made plain.

Another second and a figure had crossed in the dim light that came from one of the windows. It was a rather undersized figure, Grey thought, but its attitude was crouching, almost creeping, and he might be deceived. Quickly a hand went to the cord loops at either side of the casements and dropped the curtains, and now the room was devoid of even the dim illumination from the street lamps. Then again, for a heart-beat, there was a blade of light visible as the visitor's arm shot quickly between the lowered window hangings and drew cautiously together the open sashes, first one and then the other.

The steps now approached the bed—very slowly, haltingly, as though the intruder stopped at each footfall to listen. Grey waited, with every muscle tense, his nerves a-strain, wondering, speculating as to this night prowler's next move. For a little while his approach ceased and the suspense grew maddening. The man had evidently halted in the centre of the room. Then there came the faintest tinkle of glass touched to glass, so faint that the ticking of the clock made question whether it was not imagination; and then the stealthy stepping was resumed, but more nearly silent than before, until the man in the bed, with heart pounding, teeth shut tight and breath indrawn and held, knew that the other was there beside him—leaning in over him, between the curtains, with a hand outstretched....

Blindly, into the pitch dark, with all its power of nerve and muscle, Grey's clenched fist shot upward just as a cloth, wet with a liquid so suffocatingly volatile as to stagger him for the instant, dropped on his face. He heard a startled cry, half moan, half groan, and then a crash as a body reeled backward and, losing its balance, toppled over a chair. On his feet in a flash, Grey made haste to follow up his advantage. His foot touched his fallen assailant and he flung his full weight down upon him, groping wildly in the dark to find his arms and pinion them. But the fellow wriggled like a worm—twisting agilely, squirming from under his clutch—and his arms evaded capture. Locked in a desperate embrace they rolled over and over, now half rising to their knees, now thrown back again, upsetting tables and chairs, pounding their heads stunningly on floor and wall, clutching at each other's hair, gripping each other's throats—a wrestling match in which science had neither time nor place; a struggle for capture on the part of one, and for escape on the part of the other.

Grey was the stronger of the two, the heavier, the more muscular, but his foe was all elasticity, wiry, resilient, untiring, indomitable. The minutes passed without any apparent advantage to either. The smaller man was swearing in four languages and Grey was breathing hard. The noise they were making, as they rose and fell and overturned furniture, was thunderous. Each moment Grey expected the house would be awakened and assistance would arrive. Perspiration was pouring from his every pore; his pyjamas were in ribbons, his body and limbs half naked. Vainly he strove to strike and stun his adversary. His blows were dodged as if by instinct and his knuckles were bleeding where they had come in contact with the floor.

At length he succeeded in laying hold of the fellow's face, his nose and mouth in his iron grasp, but instantly the jaws wrenched open and then closed savagely with Grey's finger between viciously incisive teeth. A cry of pain escaped him as for the smallest moment a wave of faintness swept over him, and then he felt his antagonist slipping sinuously from under him and he grabbed wildly for a fresh hold. He caught a wrist and tried to cling to it, but the teeth were cutting to the bone, grinding on the joint, and the wrist slid through his grasp and the head followed in a twinkling. He rolled over and lunged out again, but the steely jaws had at that instant released his mangled finger, and even as he was striving to reach, struggling pantingly to his knees, he heard the door open quickly and he knew that he was alone.

He sank back to a sitting posture, breathing hard and deeply, but the air seemed suddenly to have grown thick and foul and choking, and he clambered to his feet and sought in the darkness for a window. Presently the touch of the curtains rewarded him. He thrust them frantically aside, pushed open the sashes and then dropped down again with his head and shoulders far out over the balcony, drinking in the cool, fresh air of the very early morning.

And it was here, in this position, a minute later that Johann, who had after considerable deliberation decided to investigate the cause of the disturbance, found him pale and exhausted, with the remnants of his pyjamas spattered with blood from his bleeding finger.

"Oh, Herr Arndt," he cried, in perturbation, "what has happened? Have you tried to kill yourself? Oh, it is suffocating here! The gas—the room is full of gas."

Johann helped Grey to his feet, sat him in a chair by the window, and having discovered the four gas jets of the chandelier which depended from the ceiling in the centre of the room turned full on, he turned them off, opened the other window and threw wide the door to effect a draft. Then he lighted the candles and returned to make an inventory of his master's injuries.

"I'm not very much hurt, Johann," Grey assured him; "but it was a pretty tough scrimmage while it lasted, and the brute did give my finger a biting. He had teeth like a saw and jaws like a vise. His original idea was asphyxiation, I suppose. He fancied I was asleep and that he would make it my last. By the way, look in the bed over there. You'll find a chloroformed handkerchief, I think."

"And was it for robbery, do you imagine, Herr Arndt, that he came?" Johann asked, as he went toward the bed.

"God knows," Grey answered. "It looks rather professional when a fellow unlocks your door with a pair of nippers. The key was in the lock, you see."

"You did not see his face, Herr Arndt? You would not know him?"

"I'm not a cat, Johann, and I cannot see in the dark."

Then the valet hastened away to investigate, but returned without any information worth the calling. He had aroused the *portier* only to learn that the street door had not been opened in two hours either for ingress or egress. Whoever the depredator was he must either have come in early and remained hidden or have entered through some unbarred window in the rear of the hotel, probably escaping by the same means. Having made his report Johann bathed and bound Grey's finger, drew a bath for him, got out clean nightwear, remade the bed, and, just as the clock struck the half-hour after four, left him once more alone, still with the chloroformed handkerchief in his hand, which he was examining carefully for the third time. But it was merely a square piece of fine hemstitched linen without any distinguishing mark whatever. In that, certainly, there was no clue to his visitor.

But just as he was about to blow out his candles his foot trod on something hard, and he stooped and picked up a seal ring. It was very heavy and richly chased, and it bore an elaborately engraved coat of arms. In that last despairing clutch at the fellow's hand he had evidently stripped this from his finger—this which could not but prove damaging evidence of his identity. The heraldic device was to Grey unfamiliar, but it would be a comparatively easy matter to learn to what family it belonged. Indeed, he had a vague recollection of having noticed a ring of this pattern on the little finger of Baron von Einhard's ungloved hand the afternoon before in the hotel reading-room; but the pattern was not uncommon, and— but it was preposterous to fancy that a man of his position, no matter what Lindenwald had said, no matter what his reputation for chicanery, craft, and cunning, would personally undertake a deliberate attempt at homicide. Such impossible characters might figure in melodramas, but in real life they were out of the question. And then he looked at the ring again, turning it over and inspecting it very minutely in the light of the candle flame.

Captain Lindenwald, when he was told of the affair, was quite sure it was von Einhard even before he was shown the ring, and when that was forthcoming he was willing to swear to it. The arms, he declared, were the von Einhard arms, and the ring could have been worn by no one save the Baron himself. He was for putting the matter in the hands of the police and thus avoiding future dangers, but after a little deliberation he realised that such a course would be impracticable. For the present it was absolutely necessary, he knew, to reveal nothing as to his and his charge's whereabouts. Too much was known already; and general publicity, even though it put von Einhard where he could do no personal harm, would more greatly imperil the carrying out of the plans that were indispensable.

This, at least, was the impression he conveyed to Grey, though he was, as usual, most guarded in his choice of words. Never yet, the American observed, had he directly spoken of his mission, nor had he once so much as intimated to him that he knew him as other than Herr Max Arndt. That he was a crown prince *en route* to the bedside of his dying sire Captain Lindenwald had zealously refrained from uttering save to a third party under stress of unusual circumstance, and then in a tone so low that he could not reasonably be expected to hear.

"If I may be permitted," the Captain requested, "I will keep this ring for a little. I may run across von Einhard, and I should like to give him this one hint that his attempt on your life is known to us."

But for some reason which he could not define Grey demurred.

"I have a whim to wear it," he said, replacing it upon his finger; and Lindenwald made no further plea.

VIII

It was deemed best not to mention the incident of the night to Miss von Altdorf, and on their way to the Gare St. Lazare that morning Grey accounted for his bandaged finger by the subterfuge of having caught it in a door. He was not altogether satisfied with the spot chosen for the day's outing. Had he been allowed unaided to make the choice he would undoubtedly have selected a resort of quite different character, but the girl had expressed a wish to visit Louis XIV's "*Abîme des dépenses*," and he had without demur acceded to her desire. After all, to be alone with her and thus gather from her knowledge as much information as possible concerning the mystery that surrounded him was his prime object, and for this purpose Versailles offered as propitious a background as Bougival or Croissy or a dozen other places that he personally would have preferred.

The day, washed clear and brilliant by the rain of yesterday, was not uncomfortably warm, and, though the maimed finger ached distractingly at times, Grey, in spite of his misgivings, found the little jaunt delightfully diverting. The Fraülein had shaken off much of her melancholy of the previous evening, and her mood was cheerful, if not merry. Her appreciation, which was mingled with a joyousness almost childish, was especially gratifying to her companion. Everything she saw interested her, and her comment, while invariably intelligent, was so unaffected and ingenuous as to be ofttimes amusing.

When, after *déjeuner* at the Café de la Comédie, they had come out upon the terrace of the palace and stood overlooking the quaint, solemn, old-fashioned gardens, cut up into squares and triangles and parallelograms and ornamented with statues and vases and fountains arranged with monotonously geometric precision, her face shone with pleasure for a moment and then a shadow crossed it.

"Are all landscape gardeners atheists?" she asked, naïvely.

"I'm sure I don't know," Grey replied, smiling; "I've never investigated their religious beliefs."

"Well, the one who designed all this," she added, with a sweep of her hand, "had very little respect for God's taste."

And later, as they sauntered through room after room and gallery after gallery of the palace, with their interminable succession of paintings and sculptures, she was much impressed by the pictured ceilings.

"I wonder why they put their best work where one must break one's neck to see it?" she queried; and then she laughed. "Do you suppose it was to encourage the kings and queens and other grandees to bear in mind their exalted position and to hold their heads high?"

Grey had thus far refrained from broaching the subject which had inspired the excursion. He had chosen first of all to study the girl and gauge her character. Over her presence in the little party of questionables in which he had so unexpectedly found himself he was much perplexed. It seemed scarcely reasonable to suppose that she was not in some way involved in the plot, but whether actively or passively, with knowledge or without, was, or at least might be, open to question. He certainly could gather no indication from her attitude, her manner, or her utterance that she was other than artless and sincere. She appeared, in fact, uncommonly simple-hearted, straightforward, and guileless, and, after weighing the evidence, he reached the conclusion that if she had a place in the scheme of his enemies it was most assuredly without her ken or connivance. It was nevertheless clear that she must be innocently aware of much that he wished eagerly to know, and, as they wandered over the palace together, from the sumptuously decorated *Salles des Croisades*, reflecting in picture, trophy and souvenir the conquest of Jerusalem and the Holy Sepulchre, to the magnificent *Galerie des Glaces*, with its many high-arched windows and glittering, gilt-niched mirrors, he ponderingly strove to outline some course of procedure that would yield him what he desired and yet not reveal his own delicately fragile position.

It was not, however, until they had finished their inspection of the palace and had passed out into the gardens by the *Cour des Princes* that an opportunity offered to make trial of the plan he had conceived. They had strolled under the orange trees beside that long stretch of velvet lawn towards what is known as the basin of Apollo and had found seats on the marble coping of the fountain. As they sat there facing each other amid the perfume of the flowers and the spice of the shrubbery, the balmy breath of summer fanning their cheeks and the genial glow of a tempered June sun bathing them, the girl's eye fell for the first time upon the ring on Grey's little finger, and she gave an involuntary start of surprise.

"Oh, is it you, then?" she cried, and there was something of awe in her voice, though her eyes were smiling. "But no," she added, quickly, "that cannot be. I do not understand, Uncle Max."

"Nor I, child," Grey replied, smiling back at her. He had not observed her glance, and her exclamation had startled him. She took his hand in her long, white, rose-tipped fingers and held it up before his eyes, the ring glinting in the sunshine.

"That!" she said. "What does it mean, your wearing it?"

"Mean?" he hesitated, wondering. "Why should it mean anything? Has not a gentleman a right to wear a ring if his fancy runs that way?"

"Oh, yes, of course; some rings; but no ordinary gentleman has a right to wear that one."

"But suppose I am not an ordinary gentleman?" he pursued. "Suppose I have a title and bear arms, have I not a right to engrave those arms upon gold and wear them on my finger?"

She looked at him very seriously from out her deep-set, long-lashed eyes of purplish blue, and then she said:

"But it is the ring of the Crown Prince. And you are not the Crown Prince. If you were you could not be my uncle."

Grey's heart leaped. His decision had been confirmed. She was not trying to put him on a throne to which he had no more right than those workmen who were repairing the stone margin of the great canal a hundred yards away. Yet, at the same time, she had filled him with a new perplexity. It was evident that the ring was quite familiar to her. Therefore it could hardly be von Einhard's, and Lindenwald's assertion must not only have been false but knowingly false, and with an object. If the Fraülein von Altdorf knew the ring as the Crown Prince's ring, Lindenwald must also have known it as such. It was for that reason he did not wish Grey to keep it. He feared, probably, just such a revelation as had come about. These points were plain enough, but the whole intricate problem was growing more and more involved. Its likeness to a maze again recurred. With every effort to extricate himself he seemed to get further and more bewilderingly entangled. And once more he was tempted to leave the path, which seemed to turn and turn again on itself, and to cut his way through thicket and underbrush regardless of consequences.

"What a wise Fraülein it is!" he replied, after a pause. "What you say is very true. If I am the Crown Prince I am not your uncle, and if I am your uncle I am not the Crown Prince. Now which would you prefer to have me?"

"Oh, for your sake," she answered, quickly, "I'd rather you were heir to the throne; but for my sake I'd rather you were my uncle."

"But not being able to be both, suppose you should learn that I am neither?" he queried, laughing.

"But you are," she protested, with conviction. "You are my uncle, that is a fact."

"How do you know?" Grey asked. The situation was growing interesting; disclosures were imminent, and they were coming quite naturally without his having had to resort to the plan he had mapped out.

"How does one ever know such things?" she replied, a little annoyance in her tone. "You were my Great-uncle Schlippenbach's nephew and I am your niece. I call you Uncle Max and you call me Minna."

"Ah, yes, that is very true," Grey went on, banteringly, and he remembered what O'Hara had told him of how they had met in London a week after his setting foot on English soil; "but you never saw me in your life until two months ago. Do you remember how we first met?"

"I have a very vivid recollection of it. It was at dinner at the Folsonham, in London. I wore a pale green frock. And poor Great-uncle Schlippenbach said: 'Minna, my dear, this is your Uncle Max, who hasn't seen you since you were a baby.'"

"And what else did he say?"

"Oh, I don't remember all the conversation."

"Did he say anything about where we were going, and what we were going for?"

"I don't think he said anything then. But you must remember. You were as much there as I was."

"Ah, but I was not listening," Grey pleaded, his eyes a-twinkle. "I had something better to do."

"What was that, pray?"

"I had my pretty niece to look at."

The rose in Minna's cheeks deepened and her eyes fell shyly.

"Now you are teasing me again," she said.

Grey turned an uninterested gaze for a brief space on the sun-god and his chariot which, surrounded by tritons, nymphs, and dolphins, rose in heroic proportions from the centre of the basin.

"I never knew much of my Uncle Schlippenbach," he ventured, after a little; "tell me about him."

"You should know more than I," the Fraülein returned. "You were in New York with him while I was in England."

"Yes, I know," her companion went on, as he took a cigarette from his case and struck a match, "but I don't mean intimately, personally. Tell me a little of his history."

"Everybody knew he was eccentric."

"Of course."

"Otherwise he would never have left Budavia. Just think of what he gave up!"

"That's just it," Grey interposed, eagerly. "What did he give up? I've heard stories, to be sure, but I don't know that I ever had the truth of it."

"Oh, I've heard it a hundred times," Minna responded, digging the point of her parasol into the gravel. "You see, he was tutor to the Court. He had taught King Frederic about all there was to teach, and when His Majesty outgrew school books—of course he wasn't His Majesty then, but His Royal Highness the Crown Prince—Great-uncle Schlippenbach accompanied him on the grand tour. They visited every court in Europe and then went over to Africa and Turkey in Asia, and I don't know where else. Then when Frederic succeeded to the throne, Great-uncle Schlippenbach was still retained, and after a while, when a little prince was born to Queen Anna, he was constituted a sort of kindergarten-professor to the royal infant."

"In other words, a mental wet-nurse," suggested Grey.

"Yes, exactly. I think he taught him to say 'bah' and 'boo' and 'gee-gee' and 'moo-cow'—or rather their German equivalents—and led him gloriously on to the alphabet. Then, just as he was beginning to spell nicely in words of three letters, something happened. Nobody ever knew just exactly what it was, but Great-uncle Schlippenbach took offence. Her Majesty, Queen Anna, it seems, was to blame. He brooded over the matter for weeks and months, growing more and more incensed, more and more bitter. In vain King Frederic tried to mollify him. He was very fond of Great-uncle Schlippenbach, and he wanted to smooth matters over, but the royal tutor was not to be pacified. He broke out in a torrent of rage, recounting his fancied wrongs and declaring that he had wasted the best years of his life in a hopeless effort to grow flowers of intellect from barren soil. The German Emperor would have had him behind the bars for *lèse-majesté*, but King Frederic only laughed and offered him a baronetcy. But Great-uncle Schlippenbach scorned the offer. Having spoken his mind, he packed his boxes and left the Court, left Kürschdorf, left Budavia, left Europe and went to America to begin life anew. That was twenty-five years ago, and he was forty years old."

"And the poor little Crown Prince had to learn his words of four letters from someone less gifted, eh?"

"Dear only knows from whom he ever did learn them," Miss von Altdorf continued. "He disappeared the very next week after Great-uncle Schlippenbach."

"Disappeared?" repeated Grey.

"Oh, yes, you remember that, surely. He was abducted, you know. Why, that's a part of the history of your own country. That's why there's so much excitement now over rumours of his turning up at this late day. Oh, dear, Uncle Max, why will you tease me so? You made me tell you that whole story, and I'm sure you knew it quite as well as I."

Grey laughed joyously.

"I love to hear you talk," he told her, his gaze lingering fondly on her blushing face. "And so," he added, "they are looking for the kidnapped baby to reappear a man and claim his own? Is that it?"

But she was silent, her eyes downcast.

"Won't you answer me?" he pleaded.

"I won't again tell you what you already know," she answered, a little petulantly.

"But I don't know about this ring, really," Grey urged. "Tell me about it. What has it got to do with the stolen Crown Prince?"

Minna looked up, regarding him searchingly.

"Where did you get it?" she asked.

"I found it," he answered, quite truthfully.

"In a jewel casket, within a great iron chest, inside an ordinary travelling box?" she cross-questioned.

The significance of the description was not lost on her hearer.

"No," he returned, frankly, "not in anything at all. On the floor of my room."

Her eyes were round with surprise.

"And how did it come there?"

"I cannot imagine. That is why I'd like you to tell me what you know of it."

"And before you found it on the floor of your room you had never seen it?"

"Never. I swear it by the sun-god yonder."

"My great-uncle never showed it to you—never told you of it?"

"Never," Grey repeated.

"He showed it to me in London," she confessed, reaching out for the finger it adorned, "and told me all about it. It seems that when he left Budavia it had in some way got in with his effects. He did not find it until a year or more afterward. It had belonged to the King before his coronation, and to his father before him, and to his grandfather before that. The arms are those of the Prince of Kronfeld. The Crown Prince is always, you know, the Prince of Kronfeld."

"And as the little Prince of Kronfeld had been kidnapped and Uncle Schlippenbach did not know where to find him, he simply put the ring away for safe-keeping, eh?" asked Grey, quizzically.

"He was taking it back to Kürschdorf when he died," Minna answered, with rebuke in her tone. "As soon as he heard that the Crown Prince had been found he started. He wished, he said, to put it on his finger with his own hand. 'His Royal Highness will probably travel *incognito*,' he said to me, 'but I shall know him; and when we meet I shall give him the ring. When you see it worn you will know that the wearer is the Crown Prince.'"

"And when you saw it on my finger you thought—just for a moment—that I was he, didn't you, Minna? But then, as I am your uncle I cannot be the Prince of Kronfeld, so we will take it off and wear it no more," Grey concluded, slipping the golden circlet from his finger and stowing it away in a pocket of his waistcoat.

"But what I should like to know," continued the Fraülein, "is how it came on the floor of your room?"

"And so should I," her companion echoed; "how it got out of the casket, and the iron chest, and the travelling box."

Presently the sound of many shuffling feet was borne to their ears, accompanied by the discordant piping of high-pitched voices, and turning their heads they saw approaching an army of tourists with a gesticulating, haranguing guide in the lead.

"It's a case of 'follow the man from Cook's,'" Grey observed, annoyed at having their privacy invaded. "We had better stroll on."

They walked rapidly for a while, keeping always to the right, until they were out of sight and sound of the disturbing company, and then they dawdled from terrace to terrace; leaned over lichen-stained marble balustrades to see their reflections in the dark, silent pools; loitered on banks of mossy turf beneath the shade of towering trees; stopped to admire, to criticise, and not infrequently to laugh over the sculptures that dotted the way, and came out at length upon an avenue, long and straight and level and gleaming white in the afternoon sunshine.

"You want to see the Trianons, of course," Grey suggested to the girl. "I know you are familiar with many of the events that took place there."

And so, turning to the left, they sauntered on until they came to the one-story horse-shoe shaped villa that Louis XIV built for Madame de Maintenon. But Minna was tired of sight-seeing, and the porcelains and the pictures proved alike uninteresting. The Petit Trianon pleased her much better because of its associations with Marie Antoinette, who had been one of her school-girl heroines, and over its delightful English-looking garden she grew enthusiastic.

They strolled along the winding paths, dallied on the shore of the funny little artificial lake, and rested for a while in the *"Temple de l'Amour."* The number of visitors, however, was to both of them a disturbing influence. They would have liked the place to themselves, but they were at every turn running into couples and parties whose presence, as Grey put it, "spoiled the picture."

They had just emerged from that group of homely, quaint cottages in a far corner of the garden where the fair ladies of Louis's Court were wont to play at peasant life, when the rippling laughter of women and the more hearty if less musical merriment of men broke jarringly upon their hearing.

"Can't we have some milk at the *vacherie Suisse?*" Grey heard a woman's voice ask in the English of the well-bred.

And then a man rejoined:

"Milk! What for? There's still an unopened case of champagne in the coach."

Again the laughter echoed, but nearer. The little company were coming towards them, hidden by the shrubbery. A second later and they came into view—a tall, large woman with brilliant auburn hair, in gown and hat of pale lavender; a middle-aged man, red-faced and well-groomed; a dainty little dark woman, all in red, with a tall, dark man in grey, and then—Grey went white as the whitest cloud overhead, for Hope Van Tuyl was approaching, and with her was the young man from the Embassy whom he had seen yesterday at the hotel. And there was Frothingham, too, whom he had not recognised at first glance; and it was Nicholas Van Tuyl, he saw now, who was with the red-haired woman in the lead.

For a second he halted, undecided, a powerful impulse urging him to speak to the woman he loved, at all hazards. His lips were framing words, his eyes were beaming, his hand was half way to his hat, before his judgment came to the rescue—and held him; told him that it would be folly, that now as never before it was his duty to maintain his disguise and thereby eventually establish his innocence. His eyes cooled, his teeth closed on his embryo utterance, his hand dropped to his side.

"Carey Grey!"

Hope's voice rang out suddenly above the babble of the party. She had seen him and recognised him. The others had passed on. Only she and Edson were there beside him. With an effort that cost him the most poignant torture he ever suffered he turned to Minna, murmuring words that had no meaning and walked heedlessly by.

Edson caught Miss Van Tuyl's trembling arm.

"Sh!" he warned, a little excitedly; "you've made a mistake. That isn't Grey."

"But"—and the colour came and went in her face and she breathed quickly—"but I know it is. I know him, I'm sure; oh, quite, quite sure. I cannot be mistaken. His hair is changed; yes, and he has a beard, but his eyes—I should always know his eyes; and"—as she stood gazing after him—

"his shoulders. There isn't another man in the world who has shoulders just like Carey Grey's."

"No other man, possibly," added Edson, "except the Crown Prince of Budavia."

IX

On the way back to Paris Grey's thoughtful silence contrasted so markedly with his cheery loquacity of the morning that Fraülein von Altdorf was led to observe:

"I do believe you're tired, Uncle Max."

"Tired?" he repeated, forcing a smile. "No, my child, not a bit. The day has been a joy. I've revelled in it. Tired! The idea! Am I a septuagenarian or am I an invalid?"

"But you haven't spoken for fifteen whole minutes."

"Haven't I, really? I suppose I was thinking."

"Of what?" she asked, mischievously.

Grey hesitated a little moment.

"Of fortune and misfortune," he answered, gravely; "of Fate and the pranks she plays; of life and its inconsistencies; of right and wrong and rewards and punishments; of love and hatred and jealousy; of fair women and brutal, selfish men; of a hundred and one things more or less interesting and absorbing."

"Oh, you *were* busy!" the girl exclaimed. "I don't wonder you didn't hear my question. Altogether I have asked it three times."

"I beg your pardon," he pleaded contritely; "that was very rude of me. Won't you ask it once more?"

They had a compartment to themselves and were seated opposite each other. The train had just left Asnières and was crossing the Seine.

"I was wondering whether you noticed the lady we passed in the garden of the Petit Trianon. I don't believe you did."

"We passed many ladies," Grey temporised; "I can't say that I noticed them all."

"Oh, but this one was very beautiful," she insisted. "She had such colouring and such lovely brown eyes, and I think she thought she recognised you."

"Why didn't you tell me at the time?" he asked, striving to appear unconscious.

"Why didn't I? That's a nice question. I nudged you and I tried to catch your eye; and, after we had gone on a few steps I begged you to look back, but you wouldn't heed me. Oh, you were thinking very hard just then. Was it about fair ladies and brutal, selfish men, do you imagine?"

"Probably," Grey answered. "I'm sorry I was so rude." And once more he relapsed into meditative silence.

Very bitter indeed was his self-condemnation. If he could have had a second more in which to make his decision he would have decided differently. Of that he was sure. It may have been that he took the course of wisdom, but wisdom and love have been enemies since time began, and where his allegiance was due there he had proved traitor. He contrasted his selfishness with her loyalty, and his ready willingness to conclude that she believed ill of him with her now proved steadfastness, even to the disregard of place and circumstance. He had metaphorically given her a curse for a caress, and he mentally and emotionally scourged himself for his brutality. The suggestion that desperate ills require desperate remedies—that it was necessary to be cruel that he might be kind—presented itself, but he refused to admit that it had any application. He was consumed by a desire to make reparation, to wipe out this blot of cowardice with some recklessly bold bit of bravery. He would go to her hotel—the Van Tuyls always stopped at the Ritz—and regardless of consequences he would present himself, explain all, and, in abject abasement, beseech her pardon. This, he argued, was the very least he could do. But when he reached this conclusion doubts assailed him and robbed him of what little peace he had garnered. Would she receive him? What right had he to expect that she could permit him to speak to her, now that he had repulsed her—cut her in the presence of her friends and further insulted and humiliated her by appearing more than interested in another woman—and a very young and very pretty woman, too? He most assuredly could have no just cause for complaint should she adopt such an attitude. She had indicated clearly enough that as long as only newspaper reports were his accusers she was willing to await his side of the story, but when she had given him an opportunity to defend himself, and he had chosen to ignore it and herself as well, was it in reason to hope for any further forbearance?

It was in this mood that Grey's return from Versailles was accomplished; in this ill-temper with himself and this doubt of being able to undo what he looked on as a more dire menace to his happiness than all the charges of defalcation and embezzlement and all the dangers of extradition.

When at length he and Miss von Altdorf reached the Hôtel Grammont they found O'Hara awaiting them. He came running out to the *fiacre* and gave a hand to the young woman, assisting her to alight.

"Where on earth have you been?" he asked, smiling; but Grey caught a note of concern in his voice.

"To Versailles, for the day," the Fraülein answered, gaily. "And oh, such a lovely day, too! I've enjoyed every minute of it."

"Didn't they tell you?" Grey asked. "Lindenwald knew."

"I haven't seen him."

"Johann knew."

"I haven't seen Johann either."

It was not until the two men were together in Grey's room that O'Hara broke his news.

"They've cleared out," he said, bluntly. "What do you think of that for a rum go?"

Grey, who had been drawing off his gloves, stopped midway in the process.

"Cleared out!" he repeated, in astonishment. "Who have cleared out? What do you mean?"

"The whole crew," declared O'Hara, "Lindenwald and Lutz and Johann. I understood at first that you and the Fraülein had gone with them, but the *portier* told me that you and she had started earlier and that your traps were still here."

"But they?" Grey pursued, eagerly. "Where have they gone? Did they leave no word?"

"Devil a word," returned the Irishman. "They paid their bill—that is, the Captain did—and departed, kit and all."

"What does it mean?"

"That's what I'd like to know."

Grey drew off his other glove.

"They're frightened," he decided; "they have grown suspicious. They never knew at what minute they would be pounced on. Their plot was clear enough. What they wanted to do was to palm me off as the Crown Prince of Budavia and put me on the throne when the King dies, as he is going to, if he has not already."

"What rot!" exclaimed O'Hara. "Have you gone clean daft? What would be their object? How could they hope to do it?"

"I don't know anything about their object," Grey continued, calmly; "that's still a puzzle to me; but they might hope for a lot with me in the condition I was in a few days ago. I apparently did their bidding to their utmost satisfaction."

"It's very improbable," the Irishman insisted; "you'll never be able to make any one believe it."

"Won't I?" the American demanded. "Well, then, wait and see. I've learned a lot since I saw you last. As much as I've told you is very plain. I have witnesses to prove it. And the other proofs—my God! What do you suppose has become of that box at the Gare du Nord? I sent Lutz for the check or receipt last night, and he never brought it. And this ring!" he went on, talking more to himself than to his companion, "it was in that box. Of course it was. And—" He ceased speaking—his thoughts were coming now too rapidly for words—and stood with lips pressed and eyelids drawn, gazing through his lashes into space.

He was satisfied that someone—he suspected it was Lutz—had got the box from the railway station, had rifled it, had abstracted the ring, had made so bold as to wear it. Yes, when Lutz had come in answer to his summons of the previous evening, he was wearing it even then. It must have been too large for him. He had been nervous, his hands had been twitching, and it had dropped from his finger, and—but no; could it be possible? Was it—*was* it Lutz who had returned in the early morning with intent to smother him? Was it he with whom he had wrestled? Was it from his hand that he had stripped this heirloom of the Budavian Court? And Lindenwald's assurance that it bore the von Einhard arms? What could that mean, other than that Lindenwald was in league with Lutz and striving to shield him? And now their flight....

"Will you kindly tell me whether you are subject to these attacks?" asked O'Hara, interrupting his train of thought. "If I'm to be your lieutenant and serve in your campaign, it strikes me that I should have your full and entire confidence, and yet you are keeping something from me."

"I'll tell you everything after dinner," Grey consented. "We'll have a council of war and we'll map out a plan of action."

When O'Hara had run away to dress, promising to meet Grey and the Fraülein in a private room of the Café Riche at seven-thirty and dine with them, the American's thoughts reverted to his resolution to see Hope Van Tuyl at all hazards. The disappearance of Lindenwald and the others, however, had again somewhat altered the situation. It was now more than ever necessary that he retain his freedom in order to track and run down the fugitives, and he recognised the risk he took in going to a hotel patronised largely by Americans and sending up a card bearing his real name. Once more his judgment was in the ascendency—wisdom had gained a slight advantage over the little blind god.

Sitting down at his table Grey took up a pen and wrote:

MY DARLING: For the last two hours I have been in purgatory. What must you think of me? I would come to you at once if I could, but it is impossible. Tomorrow morning, though, I must see you. At the end of the Tuileries gardens, near the Place de la Concorde, there is, you may remember, a grove of trees. Arrange to be there with your maid at eleven o'clock. There will be few there at that hour.

This he despatched to the Ritz by messenger.

"Fancy Captain Lindenwald going off!" cried Minna, as, promptly at twenty minutes past seven, she joined Grey in the drawing-room. "Where has he gone, do you suppose? And Lutz, too, and even Johann."

"They've gone to the seaside over Sunday," was Grey's jesting reply. "Paris was getting too warm for them."

"But," she protested, at fault, "I understood we were all to start for Kürschdorf tomorrow night."

"Were we? Who said so?"

"Captain Lindenwald, last evening."

"Well, Captain Lindenwald has changed his plans."

"It is certainly very mysterious," she concluded, perplexedly. "I couldn't believe it when the chambermaid told me." And the great solemn eyes were graver than usual.

When, after dinner, they returned to the hotel, Grey's glance detected a telegram in the rack addressed to the decamping Captain and he made haste to appropriate it. A little later, in his room, he handed it to O'Hara.

"It may be of service," he said, significantly. "I don't much like prying into another man's affairs, but in this case his and mine are, in a way, identical."

The Irishman nodded.

"We'll keep it until you've told me all you know without it," he suggested, taking out a briarwood pipe and filling it, "so drive ahead, lad, and don't omit any details."

And then Grey told his story, beginning with the glimpse of von Einhard, on the Boulevard St. Martin; following with the visit of Edson and the overheard announcement that he, Grey, was the Crown Prince Maximilian; the reappearance of the Baron; Lutz's suspicious demeanour; the attempt on his life; the finding of the ring; the ring's history; and, finally, his own deductions.

O'Hara listened attentively, blowing great clouds of smoke from under his red moustache. Occasionally he interrupted with a question. When the recital was concluded he got up and extended his hand.

"Well done, man," he exclaimed; "you have been making hay in sun and rain alike. I wonder if we could lay our hands on this Baron von Einhard. It seems to me that he is just the chap we want to make friends with."

"I dare say he is still hanging about," the American replied; "he probably has not lost sight of me. I'd know him if I saw him again. We'll have a look in at the cafés a little later. And now about Lindenwald and the others. Didn't the *portier* know which way they went?"

"No, they hailed a couple of passing *fiacres*, and he didn't hear what directions were given."

Grey tore open the telegram which O'Hara had tossed onto the table. It was dated Kürschdorf. "The King is dead," it read; "wire when you will be here," and it was signed, "Ritter."

He pushed it across to the Irishman, remarking:

"He probably had that news from some other source before he left."

"You think it hastened him?"

"In a way, yes. At least it directed him," Grey said, with conviction.

O'Hara looked at him inquiringly.

"You surely don't imagine the three of them have gone to Kürschdorf?" he blurted, in a tone of surprise.

"I do mean that exactly."

"But why there, of all places? If Lindenwald is expected to bring the Crown Prince with him he surely wouldn't go there empty-handed. What excuses could he make?"

"I don't pretend to conjecture his excuses," Grey replied, smiling, "but it seems very clear to me that Kürschdorf is his only sanctuary. There he will be with friends. Whatever he says is likely to be believed. If he fled elsewhere he would be in constant danger of arrest. His very flight would be evidence of his guilt."

O'Hara nodded.

"You're probably right," he acquiesced; "anyway he turned he had to take chances, and Kürschdorf must have looked to him the least dangerous. What do you propose to do?"

"Follow him," Grey answered, promptly. "Take the Orient Express tomorrow night."

"And once we are there; what then?"

"The Crown Prince claims the throne."

O'Hara put down his pipe and sat staring in amazement.

"Claims the throne?" he repeated, "the Crown Prince?"

"The Crown Prince claims the throne." Grey reiterated it with calm decision.

"You mean that *you* will claim the throne?" the Irishman persisted, still perplexed.

"Precisely."

The dragoon guard got up and walked the length of the room, smoking very hard.

"That's a dangerous business," he said, as he came back and stood with the tips of his fingers resting on the table, "a very dangerous business."

"There's no other way in God's world to find out who are in the plot," Grey returned, grimly.

"I don't quite see—" O'Hara began, but the American interrupted him.

"I haven't mastered all the details myself," he said, "but that's the kernel of the nut we're cracking. Perhaps von Einhard can aid us. He must know the conspirators, and he can give us the names of the men into whose hands we are supposed to play. I have a suspicion that the Budavian Minister here in Paris is one of the lot. But it won't do to take that for granted. Otherwise I'd see him before leaving."

"I have been thinking over the idea of consulting the Baron," O'Hara ventured, after a pause. "Suppose he won't believe you?"

"Oh, but he will," the other insisted; "I'll make it quite clear to him that I am an American and that I'm a victim and not an aspirant for kingly honours, except in so far as goes to set matters right and bring the guilty to justice."

"It's a risk that you take there, lad," the Irishman argued; "the more I think of it the bigger it looks. He's just as likely to fancy it's only a game of yours to throw him off the scent and secure your own ends. I don't believe Lindenwald exaggerated his shrewdness. I've heard of him myself."

Grey rose, leaned over the table and took a cigarette from a tray.

"Come," he said, as he struck a match, "we're liable to find him about this time."

During the past twenty-four hours he had experienced a gradual reawakening of faculties that had previously lain dull or dormant. His five months of lost memory had had an after-effect in what he could only describe as a mental thickness. His thoughts had run slowly and sluggishly; he had lacked keenness of perception and the ability to draw deductions; he had been all the while conscious of a timidity, an indecision, a hesitation, a tendency to rely upon others, against which he strove with but little effect. His actions were dictated by outside suggestion rather than by his own judgment. And with this, too, was a contrasting dignity of demeanour unnatural to him, and all the more annoying in that it was, he knew, superficial and at discord with his temperament.

The clearing of his brain, the reassertion of his naturally alert mentality, the recovery of his self-reliance, were now becoming evident; but that unwonted, and to him unwelcome, exaggeration of dignity in his carriage and demeanour gave no sign of deserting him.

O'Hara observed the change and delighted in it. The soldier in him could find only admiration for the manner in which Grey had risen mentally in one day from a subaltern to a commanding officer; and the dignified, distinguished air which had seemed, he once thought, a little incongruous appeared now as most fitting and admirable.

Together they went in search of the Budavian Baron. Into one café after another they wandered, but always without success. They encountered acquaintances by the dozen—men and women whom Grey and O'Hara had met since their arrival in Paris, and whom Grey had no recollection of ever having seen before—but the little, wiry, sallow-faced Italian-looking nobleman was nowhere in evidence.

It is never safe, however, to assume that a visitor to the French capital is abed and asleep simply because he cannot be found in any of the boulevard cafés around the hour of midnight.

X

AT the door of the Hôtel Grammont, Grey and O'Hara stood for some little time in conversation. As they were about to part, O'Hara asked: "You haven't a revolver, have you?"

"No," Grey answered, carelessly. "Shall I need one, do you think?"

"After your experience of last night it seems to me it would be just as well to sleep with one under your pillow."

Grey laughed.

"I don't fancy I shall be disturbed again," he said.

"I'll run over to my place and get you one," O'Hara insisted. "I shall be back in ten minutes."

As he went off at a brisk walk Grey turned into the wide passage that gave entrance to the court. The *portier* was not visible, but at the foot of the narrow stairway to the right a man who in the dim light had the appearance of one of the hotel valets, addressed him.

"Captain Lindenwald has returned, Monsieur Arndt," he said, quietly, respectfully; "he met with an accident and has come back. He begs that Monsieur Arndt will see him before retiring."

For a moment Grey stood silent in surprise.

"An accident?" he queried, recovering himself.

"Yes, monsieur. His train ran into an open switch at Villieurs. His leg is broken in two places, and he is injured internally. I will show monsieur to his room."

As he led the way to the floor above and along a passage towards the back of the house where Herr Schlippenbach's room had been, Grey marvelled over this new twist in the thread of fate. That the Captain had returned to this hotel and had sent for him argued, he thought, that there must have been some mistake or misunderstanding as to his departure. If he had meant to desert his charge he would not under any circumstances have acted in this fashion. Perhaps—indeed it was quite possible—he had left a letter which some stupid French servant had failed to deliver, or it might simply have been his intention to spend Sunday out of Paris, giving Lutz and Johann permission to take a brief holiday as well. O'Hara had said something about their luggage being gone, but that might have been an error, too.

At a turn in the passage Grey's guide halted before a door and rapped, playing, as it were, a sort of brief tattoo on the panel with his knuckles; and at the same time a waiter passed on his way to the rear stairway.

An instant later the door was opened by someone who shielded himself behind it. The man who had led the way and done the rapping stepped back, and the American, his eyes a little dazzled by the light, put a foot across the threshold. Just what followed Grey never exactly knew. A myriad brilliant, sparkling, rapidly darting specks of fire filled his vision. In his ears was a thunderous rushing sound like a storm sweeping through a forest—a swollen river churning through rocky narrows. His body seemed dropping through interminable space, gaining momentum with every foot of its fall, but shooting straight, straight downward without a swerve; the lights flashing by him, the winds roaring past him as he sped. An agony of apprehension seized him. He was going to be crushed to atoms; mangled, broken, distorted. He tried to raise his arms, to clutch at the impalpable, but they were held down as if by leaden weights. To bend a knee, to lift a foot, to cry out, were alike impossible of achievement. And then, with a crash that split his ears, that tore every joint asunder, that racked every nerve, muscle, sinew and tendon, the end came. The myriad sparks, like the countless flashing facets of countless diamonds, were drowned in blackest night and the terrifying rush of furious winds and frantic waves was hushed in a silence profound and awful—the blackness and the silence of unconsciousness.

Very gradually, but in much shorter time than he fancied, or than his assailants expected, he recovered command of his faculties and became aware that he was lying upon a couch, an improvised gag in his mouth, his arms pinioned in a most uncomfortable way at his sides, and his feet bound together with cords that cut cruelly into the flesh of his ankles. He realised then that he had been led into a trap and had been sandbagged or otherwise assaulted as he entered it. His mind was still busy with Lindenwald and his motives, he fancied at first that he was responsible for this outrage, and warily, between his lashes, with his eyes scarcely opened, he glanced about the room in search of this gallant member of the Budavian royal household.

There were, however, but two persons present, and Lindenwald was not one of them. One was the little man whom he had mistaken for a hotel valet and who had lured him to his downfall; and the other was a tall, burly, bearded fellow, with a low forehead and sinister, bloodshot eyes. The two were standing near an open window and the larger man had in his hands a thick hempen rope, one end of which Grey observed was knotted about the heavy post of an old-fashioned mahogany bedstead which stood against the opposite wall. On more careful inspection he saw that the man was deliberately making a slip knot of the pattern known as a hangman's noose. The only light in the room was that given by a single candle, but it sufficed for Grey to gather these details.

The smaller man leaned out of the window for a moment, and on drawing in his head he turned to the other with the remark:

"The carriage is there. Make haste with your knot. I'm not in love with this business."

He spoke in German and his partner replied in the same tongue.

"Have patience," he said, calmly; "it's a heavy body we've got to lower and the knot must be strong. There's plenty of time. He won't come to himself for hours, and there's no fear of anyone interrupting us now."

"Don't be too sure of that," was the reply, in a tone of nervous apprehension; "we have been here too long as it is. If we should fail at the last minute, the Baron would——"

"S—sh!" warned the other, "no names is safer. Just another wrapping now and she'll hold all right. Some wrap it seven times and some only five, but I'm giving it nine, to be sure."

He had scarcely finished the sentence when a blow, aggressive and imperious, sounded on the door. The younger man started nervously, but the other just phlegmatically lowered his work and raised his head.

"What's that mean?" he whispered.

"God knows!" the other replied, agitatedly. "What's to be done?"

"Done? Nothing. Keep still, that's all. Blow out that candle," he commanded. Though he spoke very low his voice penetrated and Grey caught every word.

Again a heavy blow struck the door, repeated blows, accompanied by a demand:

"*Ouvrez la porte!*"

The voice was O'Hara's. Grey recognised it with a thrill. He had returned with the revolver, and not finding him in his room had set out in search of him. But how, he wondered, could he have traced him here? And then he thought of the waiter he had seen in the passage, who had evidently recognised him. Yes, the waiter must have told.

Now Grey heard other voices outside. There was the shuffling, too, of many feet. Still, the men within made no sound. The candle had been extinguished and the darkness was intense.

The knocking became clamorous. There was a general ominous murmur like low growling thunder from the other side of the door.

Bang! bang! bang! resounded the blows.

"Open the door! Open at once or I'll break it down," O'Hara roared.

Grey's enforced silence and inertia were maddening. He bit at his gag, contorted his mouth, tugged at his arms, but could accomplish nothing, beyond a wriggling change of position.

"Perhaps they have gone," he heard someone say, whose voice was sonorous, "perhaps they have gone. Escaped by the window. There is no light there; and no sound."

"Stop!" It was O'Hara speaking. "Listen!"

With an effort Grey squirmed to the edge of the couch and dropped his bound body to the floor with a thud that echoed through the silent room.

"Damn him!" he heard the bigger of his two companions hiss through his teeth.

From outside there came a yell of triumph; and then a heavy, crashing, catapultian mass fell upon the fragile portal. There was a crackling, splintering sound of wood rent apart, and through the aperture thus made, in the dim light of the single gas-jet in the passage, O'Hara came plunging with half a dozen of the hotel employés at his heels.

At the same instant a head disappeared below the sill of the window, and the rope from the bedpost was stretched taut and creaking with the weight of two descending bodies.

The Irishman, crossing the room in a flash, missed the form of his prostrate friend by a hair's-breadth and dived headlong for the open casement. But quick as he was the fleeing scapegraces, realising their danger, were even more speedy. As his head shot out into the night the strain on the rope relaxed and there came up from the darkness below a patter of feet on the stone flagging of the alley. His pistol was in his hand and he fired once—twice—three times—blindly into the blackness beneath, guided only by the echo of those retreating footsteps.

Meanwhile, one of the Frenchmen—Baptiste, the waiter, by the way, who had told O'Hara that he saw Monsieur Arndt enter this room—was removing the gag from Grey's mouth, while others were cutting the cords that bound his limbs. For a moment the American's view of the Irishman's broad back was cut off by those surrounding him, but the next minute he was on his feet and—but in that instant O'Hara had disappeared. Clutching the dangling rope, he had swung himself out of the window and had slid down nimbly in pursuit.

Grey's impulse was to follow, but at the first step he reeled dizzily and would have fallen had not Baptiste thrown an arm about him and aided him to a chair. His head was aching splittingly and his legs and arms were numb. For a little while he was lost to everything save the racking torture of physical pain. Then the voluble, excited clatter of the men about him recalled him to a sense of what had happened.

"What are you standing here for?" he cried, vexedly. "Get down to the street, every one of you. Monsieur O'Hara may need you. Off, I say. Be quick!"

"But, monsieur," urged Baptiste, hanging back as the other five made a hasty exit, "is it not that monsieur would like a surgeon?"

"Surgeon be damned!" yelled Grey, excitedly. "Out with you!"

But in five minutes they were back again in augmented numbers, with O'Hara accompanied by a *sergent de ville* at their head.

"They got clean away, the beggars," the Irishman announced; and then seeing Grey very white, he exclaimed: "Are you hurt, lad? What in God's name did they do to you, the scalawags?"

"I'm only a little knocked up," the American answered, with a forced smile; "it was a pretty hard rap on the head they gave me, though."

The police officer had taken out a notebook, and now he began to ask questions. There was very little, however, that anyone could tell him. Grey described his assailants as accurately as he knew how, and gave him the benefit of his suspicions.

"By whom was the room engaged?" asked the *sergent*, addressing Baptiste; but Baptiste did not know. Then a messenger was sent to arouse the *portier*, who had been abed for an hour or more, and when at length he came in, still rubbing his eyes, the information that he gave conveyed nothing.

The room, he said, was taken that evening by a man of ordinary appearance who gave the name of Schmidt. His brother and a friend would occupy it, he told the *portier*, and he paid one day's rent in advance.

"Was the man tall or short?" asked the officer.

The *portier* shrugged his stalwart shoulders.

"I do not know," he replied.

"Was he dark or fair?"

"I cannot tell you, monsieur," he repeated; "I did not notice."

"Of what age?"

"It is impossible that I should conjecture, monsieur," with another shrug.

Grey laughed, sneeringly. "He evidently paid more than room rent," he said to O'Hara. "The Baron von Einhard is very clever."

And when, a little while after, he thought of looking through his pockets he had reason to reiterate and emphasise this opinion. Not a penny of his money had been touched; his watch and chain were still in his possession, as were indeed all of his belongings save one. The ring of the Prince of Kronfeld alone was missing.

XI

RESENTMENT—fierce, vengeful, absorbing—took possession of Carey Grey. That he should have been disgraced, dishonoured, robbed for a time of his reason and his memory, his friends made to suffer, his life put in jeopardy, and all without the slightest provocation, was an outrage so heinous that he considered no punishment too great for its perpetrators. The fact that the one who was apparently mainly responsible for the inspiration and the execution had been summoned to a spiritual tribunal to answer for his misdeeds tempered not a whit the victim's bitter animosity. Indeed, he felt that death had cheated him of what he craved as a meagre compensation for his wrongs—the opportunity to visit personally upon the arch-offender his own retribution. But if Herr Schlippenbach had been snatched from his hands by a too kindly Providence there were others remaining who should feel the weight of his relentless vengeance.

In this mood, wakeful and dreamful by turns, a cold compress on his bruised head, Grey worried through the early hours of the morning. With the first sign of the blue dawn, however, he became more composed. His meditations took on a more gentle guise; his brow, which had been wrinkled with frowns, smoothed; into his eyes came a tenderness that routed spleen, and his mouth softened its tensity of line. The day held for him a joy the anticipation of which was a benison.

After all, heaven was not wholly unkind. He had been made to suffer cruelly and undeservedly, but there was at least one compensation—the woman he loved was here, near him, in the same city; in a few hours he would meet her, talk with her, feel the warmth of her hand in his, experience the benignant sympathy of her eyes and the caressing graciousness of her voice. With the dawn had come confidence, and he smiled as he recalled his doubts of the previous afternoon. Her love was steadfast, enduring, immutable. Of this he felt assured. And her faith and loyalty were like her love. He lay for hours in blissful contemplation of the character, disposition, mind, manner and person of the woman he adored.

He recalled their first meeting at a barn dance at Newport, when she was in her débutante year; and then, an event of the following day came back to him vividly as in a picture. The scene was the polo field at Point Judith. He had just made a goal by dint of hard riding and unerring strokes, and a hurricane of applause had followed, led, it seemed to him, by a tall young woman in white, with great, shining brown eyes and flushed cheeks, who was standing up in her place atop a coach, clapping her hands in frantic delight. And this picture was followed by others—a panorama in which the same girl figured again and again—always beautiful, always smart, always gracious.

He attired himself, this fine Sunday morning, with more than usual care, despite the absence of his valet, and set forth early for the rendezvous he had chosen. Already the boulevards were alive. Many of the chairs in front of the cafés were occupied by sippers of absinthe and drinkers of black bitters. From the gratings in the sidewalks arose the appetising aroma of the Parisian *déjeuner à la fourchette*. He crossed the Avenue de l'Opéra and, turning into the rue de la Paix, was presently passing the entrance of the hotel that sheltered her who filled his thoughts—her whom he had come out to meet. A *fiacre* was at the curb, and, fancying that it might be awaiting her, he hastened his steps so that he should not encounter her in so public a place. From the summit of the Vendôme Column the imperial-robed Napoleon cast an abbreviated shadow across his path as he cut across the *place* into the rue de Castiglione. A man he did not remember bowed graciously as he passed him at the corner of the rue de Rivoli, and a little further on a somewhat showily gowned woman in an enormous picture hat, probably on her way to the Madeleine, leaned from her carriage to smile upon him. And she, likewise, was without his recollection.

At the corner of the rue Cambon he made a diagonal cut to the garden side of the street, and a minute later reached the broad and imposing Place de la Concorde in all its bravery of bronzed iron and granite fountains, sculptured stone figures, rostral columns and majestic Obelisk.

As he turned into the gardens of the Tuileries, Grey glanced at his watch to discover that the time still lacked five minutes of eleven. He looked back in expectation of seeing a cab approaching, but, though there were many crossing the place at various angles, there was none headed in his direction. He strolled off between the flower-beds into the little grove at his right. Just ahead of him he descried a figure in pink, and his heart bounded; but he overtook it only to meet disappointment. He lighted a cigarette, sat down on a bench, and dug in the gravel with his walking-stick; his eyes, though, ever on the alert, looking now one way, now another. He took out his watch again. The minute hand was still a single space short of twelve. He got up and retraced his steps towards the entrance with the object of meeting her as she came in. Again he gazed across the wide, sun-washed area of the place, but without reward, and then a dour melancholy threatened him. He was assailed by forebodings. She would not come. He had offended her beyond reparation. The day suddenly grew dull. A cloud hid the sun. The gaiety of those who passed him became offensive. The sight of a youth with his sweetheart hanging on his arm filled him with rancour. He walked back and forth irritably. He was depressed, heavy-hearted, apprehensive.

Another five minutes dragged by, with a corresponding increase in the young man's dejection. His imagination was now active. It was quite possible she had left Paris. His messenger, perhaps, had failed to deliver his note. He wondered if by any chance she might be ill.

He was standing, pensive, by the fountain, undecided whether to wait longer or to go on to the Ritz in search of her, when the rustle of skirts behind him caused him to turn.

"Ah—h!" exclaimed a laughing voice, "it is then you after all. I was not sure. I looked and I looked, but you are so changed, Mr. Grey!"

It was Marcelle, Miss Van Tuyl's maid, and at the sound of her peculiar accent Grey recognised her instantly. He realised, too, that it was she whom he had seen on the moment of his coming—the figure in the pink frock.

"Miss Van Tuyl sent this note, Mr. Grey," she went on, handing him an envelope which he noticed was unaddressed.

His spirits rose a trifle. She had not left Paris, then, and she had received his message.

"Miss Van Tuyl is not ill, I hope?" he questioned, anxiously.

"Oh, no, Mr. Grey," and Marcelle shrugged her plump shoulders and raised her black eyebrows, "but—" and she hesitated just the shade of a second "she is—oh, I fear she is most unhappy."

"Thank you very much, Marcelle," he said, ignoring her comment, though the words were as a sword-thrust, and handing her a louis. "Is there an answer?"

"I do not know, monsieur; but I think not."

Grey tore open the envelope and glanced over the inclosure.

"No," he announced, his face very set and suddenly pale. "Give my compliments to Miss Van Tuyl," he added, "that is all."

When the girl had gone he turned again into the little grove and once more found the seat under the trees where a few minutes before he had impatiently dug the gravel with his walking-stick. He sat now with his forearms resting on his thighs, the note crushed in his hand, his eyes bent, thoughtful but unseeing, on the grass across the walk.

She had refused to come to him. It was probably better, she had written, that they should not meet again. She could imagine nothing in the way of explanation that would form an adequate excuse for his action of the afternoon before. And that was all. Only five lines in a large hand.

The self-chastisement of the man was pitiless; his contrition pathetic. He was willing now to make any sacrifice, to suffer any abasement, to risk any punishment, to sustain any loss if by so doing he could gain forgiveness, achieve reinstatement in favour—aye, even attain the privilege of pleading his cause. He had been so sure of her; it had not seemed possible that she could ever be other than love and devotion and loyalty personified. Her smile was the one sun he thought would never set and never be clouded. And now she had taken this light from his life forever. With that gone, he asked himself, what else in all the world mattered? What were honour, position, credit, fortune, if she were not to share them?

He smoothed out the crumpled sheet and read it again, slowly, carefully, weighing each word, measuring each phrase, considering each sentence. And then the utter hopelessness of his expression changed. "It is probably better," he repeated, quoting from the note, and the "probably" seemed larger and more prominent than any other eight letters on the page. There was nothing absolutely final about that. It was an assertion, to be sure, but there was a lot of qualification in that "probably." And further on, she had not said: "There is nothing in the way of explanation you can offer," but "*I can imagine* nothing." He thanked God for that "I can imagine." Oh, yes, indeed, there was a very large loophole there; and so he took heart of grace, and even smiled, and got up swinging his stick jauntily. All he wanted was a fighting chance. He had won her a year ago from a score of rivals, and he would win her now from herself. And not from herself, either, for with the return of hope he felt that he would have no more stanch ally than she. It was with her sense of what was fit and becoming that he must battle—her pride and her self-esteem which he had outraged. He would go to her, bravely, as he should have done before, instead of asking her to meet him in this clandestine fashion. He had been a fool, but he would make amends and she would forgive him. Yes, he was quite sanguine now that he could win her pardon.

He retraced his steps briskly to the Place Vendôme and turned in at the Ritz with head erect and chin thrust forward. He had no cards, of course, but he scribbled "*Carey Grey*" upon a slip of paper and asked that it be sent to Miss Van Tuyl at once. And then he waited, nervously, smoking one cigarette after another, walking back and forth, sitting down, only to get up again, agitatedly, and to resume his pacing to and fro.

"Miss Van Tuyl is not at home, monsieur."

It was the *portier* who delivered the message. Grey stood for a full half-minute, staring stupidly. He had not counted upon this. He had been all confidence. That she was in the hotel he felt very certain; but she would not see him. He might have foreseen that consistency demanded this attitude of her. To send him a note one moment refusing to permit him to explain and at the next to grant him an audience was not to be expected of a young woman of Hope Van Tuyl's sterling character. There was, therefore, but one course open to him. What he had to say he must put in writing.

"I'll leave a note," he said to the *portier*; and he went into the writing-room and sat down at a table. But when he came to write he was embarrassed by the flood of matter that craved expression. There was so much to tell, so much to make clear, so much to plead that he was staggered by the contemplation. Again and again he began, and again and again he tore the sheet of paper into tiny bits. He dipped his pen into the ink and held it poised while he made effort to frame an opening sentence; and the ink dried on the nib as one thought after another was evolved only to be rejected.

For the fifth time he wrote: "My Very Dearest," and then, nettled over his laggard powers, he dove straight and determinedly into the midst of the subject that engrossed him, writing rapidly and without pause until he had finished:

"I cannot find it in my heart to question the justice of your decision," he began. "Viewed in the light of your meagre knowledge, or rather ignorance, of facts, I must look indeed very black. But I am guiltless; that I swear. Under the circumstances you must know how anxious I am to prove this, and how, in justice to you and myself, I must let no opportunity pass to discover and convict the real culprits. To have recognised you at Versailles yesterday before the man you were with would have been to ruin every chance of accomplishing what I have set out to do. Imagine, my dear, the alternative from which I had to choose. Had it been simply a question of my personal liberty, you cannot doubt which course I should have taken. I was burning to speak to you—to look into the eyes I love, to hear the voice I adore— and yet for both our sakes I had to deny myself. The child who was with me is sweet and charming, and in no way implicated in the plot against me. When you know her, as I hope you will one day, you will be very fond of her. But I can understand how the situation must have appeared to you. I would give all I have and all I hope for if I could but be with you and tell you everything. All I ask now is that you trust me. I am leaving Paris this afternoon for Kürschdorf by the Orient Express. I cannot say when I shall return. But when I do it will be to search for you, and with honour vindicated and no further need of secrecy. My heart is with you always, my darling. *'Au revoir.'*"

The letter dulled, in a measure, the keenness of Grey's disappointment and reinspired him to the accomplishment of the task that lay before him. After luncheon he had up his trunks from the hotel storeroom and with Baptiste's assistance accomplished his packing. Already O'Hara had engaged places for three on the train, for Miss von Altdorf's destination was the same as theirs. She had a married sister living in Kürschdorf, and she was most anxious to join her at the earliest possible moment.

By half-past five everything was in readiness for their departure; Baptiste had retired with a liberal tip, and Grey and O'Hara were making themselves ready for the journey. Just at this juncture there was a knock at the door, and in answer to Grey's command to enter, it swung open to reveal, bowing on the threshold, the sturdy little figure, pale face, and close-cropped yellow head of Johann.

The two occupants of the room stood astonished, their eyes wide with surprise.

"Johann!" they exclaimed together.

"Yes, Herr Arndt," said the lad, bowing again; "it is as you see—I have come back."

"Back from where, Johann?" Grey asked.

"I started for Kürschdorf with the Herr Captain Lindenwald; but I am come back from Strasburg."

"And why?" queried the American, very much puzzled.

"Because, Herr Arndt, I knew it was not right for me to be going with the Herr Captain. I was in your service, and perhaps if you were seized with madness you have all the more need of me."

"Madness!" repeated Grey, frowning. "What is this? Who said I was mad?"

"The Herr Captain and Lutz," confessed Johann, stolidly, with scarce a change of expression.

O'Hara laughed. "Oh, ho!" he shouted, dropping into a chair, "now we have it. You are mad, and so you cannot go to Budavia to claim your own."

Johann nodded; and Grey, leaning against the edge of the table, was lost for a moment in thought.

"But the Fraülein?" O'Hara questioned. "What did they say of her? Was she to be left with the madman?"

"No, Herr O'Hara; only for a little. The Herr Captain Lindenwald had arranged, Lutz told me, to have Herr Arndt taken to an asylum by the doctors and then the Fraülein was to be brought to Kürschdorf."

Grey smiled, grimly. "The doctors were the gentlemen you chased out of the window last night, Jack," he said. And then he asked of Johann: "Did they say anything of Baron von Einhard?"

"No, Herr Arndt."

"You are quite sure?"

"I have not heard of his name, Herr Arndt."

Then Johann was told of the plan of departure and was sent off to telephone for another place on the Orient Express for himself. When he returned the American said to him:

"It was very good of you, Johann, to come back."

"Ah, Herr Arndt," he returned, in a tone of appreciation, "I could not do less. Can I ever, do you think, forget that it was you who saved my life?"

Grey's surprise must have shown in his eyes, but he asked no questions. Later, however, just as they were about to start for the Gare de Strasbourg, he found himself alone with O'Hara for a moment and put the query to him:

"What is this about my having saved Johann's life?"

"You don't remember it? Oh, of course not," the Irishman answered. "Well, you had your pluck with you, lad, if you didn't have your memory. We were in that fire at the Folsonham, in Piccadilly. It happened in the early morning when the whole house was asleep, and that the death list was not larger was little short of a miracle. The front stairs were burning as Schlippenbach, the Fraülein and you and I reached them. When I got to the bottom I missed you, and looking back saw you through the smoke still standing at the top. 'For God's sake, make haste, man!' I called, 'the stairs may fall at any minute.' But you had seen a figure staggering down, half suffocated, from the floor above. Well, instead of saving yourself you went back to help that figure, which proved to be Johann. And even at that moment the staircase fell with a crash. But you caught the stumbling, dazed Budavian from out a hurricane of sparks, rushed him through a room filled with blinding smoke and climbed with him hanging limp over your shoulder out of a window onto an already burning ten-inch cornice. And there you held him, against the wall, God only knows how, until a ladder was run up and the pair of you brought safely to the street just as the cornice crumbled and went down. And, good Lord, but didn't the crowd cheer! Only fancy your not remembering anything of it!"

"I'm glad I managed it," said Grey, simply. But the story depressed him. What else had he done in those five months of somnambulism? The thought of that period and its possibilities had grown distressful to him. He had committed a great crime and he had performed a brave deed. They were the opposite poles of that world of sleep. But what other acts lay between? What other incidents of right and wrong filled the intermediate zones? He shrank from asking general questions on the subject, and speculation was as distasteful as it was futile. When, as in this instance, accident had revealed something, the result was a sort of emotional nausea.

XII

ON the platform of the Gare de l'Est, with ten minutes to spare before the departure of the Orient Express, Grey and O'Hara, with the fair Minna von Altdorf between them, strolled leisurely up and down beside the long and lugubrious train of *wagons-lit*. There was the usual bustle incident to the leaving of the great transcontinental flyer. Passengers were nervously seeking their locations; blue-overalled porters wheeling trucks piled high with trunks and boxes hurried towards the luggage vans, and others with smaller impedimenta in hand crowded on the narrow platforms of the cars and ran into the still smaller passageways upon which the compartments opened. English and American tourists unable to speak the language of the country were besieging the interpreters; friends and kinsfolk with lingering handshakes, effusive embraces, and kisses upon either cheek were bidding departing travellers farewell, and dapper-uniformed guards were at intervals repeating the stereotyped command: "*En voiture, messieurs!*" There was the distracting hissing of escaping steam, the shrill piping of whistles, the rumble and roar of arriving trains. And over all hung an atmosphere of intolerably humid heat.

O'Hara and the Fraülein were chatting animatedly, but Grey was still depressed and silent. The delay irritated him. He was impatient to be gone. For the hundredth time he was wondering whether he had said too much or too little in his letter to Hope Van Tuyl; wondering how she regarded it; whether she was still obdurate. He had not given her an address and there was no way in which she could communicate with him. He regretted this now. A word from her would be a talisman.

His memory of her as he had seen her yesterday at Versailles was very vivid. It was only a glimpse, but in that instant he had drunk in greedily the marvellous perfection of her beauty; and the picture had dwelt with him since. Sleeping and waking he could see the bronze dusk of her hair, the gentleness of her eyes, the softly flushed curve of her cheek, the tender sympathy of her mouth, the supple grace of her figure. The portrait was not new to him, to be sure—he had many times revelled in fond contemplation of those rare features—but absence had its usual effect, and it had been centuries, it seemed, since his vision had been so blessed. Against the dull, dun, grimy background of the railway station this radiant reflection was projected, clear and sharp. He saw her mentally just as he had seen her physically on the previous afternoon.

And as he gazed a miracle was wrought. For into and out of the image came and grew the reality, and he suddenly realised that she was standing before him, that in one hand he was holding his hat and that his other hand was clasping hers. All the sights and sounds of the platform died away, and he saw only her, more beautiful even than he had dreamed, her eyes alight with love, her lips smiling forgiveness.

O'Hara and the Fräulein had passed on, and he and the one woman in the world had drawn aside out of the hurry and scurry. A few steps away stood Marcelle, the maid, her interest decorously diverted.

"Oh, how good you are!" Grey was saying, his heart in his voice; "how very, very good you are!"

Her hand answered the ardent pressure of his.

"I just couldn't let you go without seeing you," she returned. "You cannot imagine what I have suffered. I tried to be brave—I tried so hard, dear; but I'm only a weak woman and my soul longed for you every minute."

What bliss it was to hear her speak! It set the man's pulses surging. His face was flushed and young and happy again, as it had not been since his awakening.

"The whole thing has been frightful," he told her, clenching his teeth at the recollection. "You haven't an idea what a net of circumstance has been thrown around me."

"Yes," she hastened, "I know—they told me you had been ill, irresponsible; that you had had brain fever or something, and—oh, Carey, why did you do that?" and she pointed to his beard.

He smiled grimly.

"I didn't do it," he answered, with emphasis. "You surely don't think I'd be guilty of such a ridiculous transformation, do you?"

"But——"

"I'll explain some day, dear heart," he interrupted her, "but there isn't time now; the train leaves in about five minutes, and I want all of that in which to tell you how very beautiful you are and how very, very much I love you."

She wore a perfectly fitting gown of white with rich lace, and a large hat of pale blue with a circling ostrich plume of the same delicate tint. Her tall and shapely figure was quite unavoidably a little conspicuous, and a target for admiring glances.

"Leaves in five minutes?" she repeated, dolorously. "But I can't let you go in five minutes. I have so much to say to you. It has been five months since I spoke to you. You must wait and take the next train—wait until tomorrow."

"If only I might!" Grey replied, his eyes in hers. "If it could only be we should never part again, never! Ah, my own, how my arms ache for you!"

"But you can stay," she urged. He was still holding her hand, and now she placed her other hand over his as she pleaded. "There is no reason why you shouldn't. What difference will twenty-four hours make? Are you going for the King's funeral? It is set for Friday, you know. We are thinking of going ourselves. Wait until tomorrow, and you and papa and I can go together."

"But, my darling," Grey protested, arguing against his inclination, "don't you see that that would be quite impossible? Your father could not afford to be seen with me. I am a supposed fugitive from justice. He would be guilty of aiding and abetting a criminal," and he smiled grimly again.

"What would he care?" the young woman demanded, airily. "He doesn't believe you guilty. He knows you are not. He has said as much. I can't let you go, dear; I can't—I won't."

"Please, please don't make it more difficult for me to part from you than it is already," he begged. "You know how much I long to have you with me, and yet another day's delay might ruin everything. I should be in Kürschdorf at this very minute."

Her eyes glistened and tears hung on her lashes.

"Why?" she asked, simply.

"All my hopes of undoing the wrong that has been done me lie in that direction," he answered, gravely. "It was a conspiracy, dear, involving men high in the Budavian government. The work of unmasking them will grow more difficult with each hour it is put off."

She gazed at him in sudden alarm.

"You are going into danger," she murmured. Her voice trembled. Anxiety was in her tone. She pressed his hands nervously, convulsively. "Tell me the truth. You are, aren't you?"

Grey laughed to reassure her.

"Not a bit, my darling," he answered, with an assumption of nonchalance; "the whole affair can, I think, be adjusted most peacefully."

For a moment she was silent, her eyes reading his thoughts.

"I'm going with you," she exclaimed, suddenly.

Grey stared at her in surprise.

"I only wish you could," he said, refusing to take her seriously, "but I don't see just how——"

"I'm going," she interrupted, determinedly. "I shan't be in the least in your way, that I promise. But I'm going. I refuse to be left behind."

"*En voiture, messieurs et mesdames!*"

The guard's command had grown imperative. The second bell had rung.

Grey pulled out his watch. It showed thirty seconds of starting time. O'Hara was standing at the car's step looking anxiously towards him. Johann was at his side, his hat deferentially raised.

"The train is now to start, Herr Arndt," he said.

The man turned to the woman he loved.

"I am going with you," she reiterated before he could speak; and she beckoned to Marcelle.

"*En voiture!*" shouted the guards.

There was no time for further protest or parley. The four crossed the platform hurriedly. Hope entered the car, her maid following; and then Grey, with O'Hara at his heels and Johann bringing up the rear, stepped from the platform of the station to the platform of the *wagon-lit*.

The third bell rang; the locomotive whistled its piping treble, gates clashed, doors slammed, and the Orient Express drew slowly and solemnly out of the hot, dingy station into the red glare of the torrid June sunset.

After the presentation of Miss von Altdorf and Lieutenant O'Hara had been accomplished Grey left Hope in their company and went in search of the conductor. As it happened, there were several berths to spare in the sleeping-car, and he arranged for the accommodation of Miss Van Tuyl and her maid. There would be no stop, however, he learned, until they reached Château-Thierry, at 8.15. From there, the conductor told him, a telegram might be sent.

Before returning to the compartment Grey lit a cigarette and stood for a few minutes in the refreshing draft that swept through the narrow passage. To have Hope with him was a joy undreamt, and yet he could not repress a little uneasiness over her action. He feared that in a calmer mood she might regret her impulsiveness as savouring too strongly of a sensational elopement. He wondered how Nicholas Van Tuyl would regard it. He was, Grey knew, the most indulgent of fathers, but his anxiety over her absence would necessarily be poignant, and there was no possible means of getting word to him of her safety until hours after he had missed her. But in spite of these reflections Carey Grey was experiencing a gratified pride in the fact that the girl had acted as she had. She was proving her love for him and her faith in him by a disregard of convention that was undeniably very flattering, particularly grateful after his recent trying experiences, and his affection for her, if possible, waxed warmer under the stimulus of appreciation.

Meanwhile the trio Grey had left to their own devices, with scarcely a word of explanation, were getting into a wellnigh inextricable tangle.

"Fancy my deciding to run off this way on the spur of the moment, without even a handful of luggage," Miss Van Tuyl had exclaimed, "but Mr. Grey and I have so much to talk about I just couldn't think of waiting another twenty-four hours, and he said he couldn't possibly stop over another day in Paris."

Minna had recognised her minutes before on the platform, as the beautiful lady she had noticed the previous afternoon at Versailles, and she had been and was still wondering how it came about that her Uncle Max had not seen her and spoken to her there. And now this mention of a Mr. Grey perplexed her. Was he in another car or another compartment? And if she had so much to say to him why had she stood talking to another man until the train was on the point of leaving? and why was she sitting here now instead of being with him?

"American women are such fun," O'Hara was saying, his cheery, ruddy face one broad smile. "I admire them awfully. They're so superbly self-reliant."

"You're an American, Miss Van Tuyl?" the Fräulein ventured. "Oh, of course. It was in America, I suppose, you met Uncle Max?"

Hope stared questioningly.

"Uncle Max?" she questioned. "I don't understand you. Who is——"

"Didn't you know he was my uncle?" the girl asked, a little embarrassed.

"Really, I—" she began again. And then O'Hara came to the rescue:

"Our mutual friend, Miss Van Tuyl. After all, what's in a name? Miss von Altdorf calls him 'Uncle Max' and you— what is your favourite pet name for him? Or is it rude of me to ask?"

"Oh, I beg your pardon," Hope implored, addressing the fair-haired girl beside her; "how stupid of me! Yes, of course;

I met him in America when we were both very young. You were with him yesterday at Versailles, weren't you? I remember you distinctly. Mr. Grey wrote me something very nice about you."

"About me? Mr. Grey?" It was the Fräulein's turn to be audibly perplexed.

"Yes, certainly, Mr. Grey wrote me about you."

"But I don't know any Mr. Grey."

O'Hara laughed aloud. Should he or should he not, he asked himself, set them right and thus end this game of cross-purposes? It was very amusing, it appealed to his native love of fun and he enjoyed it, so he concluded to let the play go on.

"Why, my dear Miss von Altdorf," Hope insisted, "do you mean to tell me that you don't know your Uncle Max's name is Grey?"

Minna's eyes were wide with amazement. Could it be possible that her uncle was known in the United States by another name? The supposition was preposterous.

"My Uncle Max's name is Arndt," she said, very decidedly. "He is my mother's brother, and my mother's name was Arndt before she married."

Hope leaned back in the hot, stuffy cushions of the railway carriage, nonplussed. This was altogether beyond her understanding. And the Fräulein, a little nettled, but triumphant, sat looking at her with something of pity in her great long-lashed blue eyes, while O'Hara on the seat opposite was bent double in a convulsion of merriment.

"I don't really see, Mr. O'Hara," Minna observed, rebukingly, a moment later, "what there is to laugh over. Would you mind telling me?"

The Irishman, who had more than a passing fondness for the girl, pulled a straight face on the instant.

"I'm sorry, Miss von Altdorf," he apologised. "It's too bad of me, isn't it? And I beg Miss Van Tuyl's pardon, too. I'd like to explain the whole blessed thing to you both, but to tell the truth, I fancy the gentleman of the mixed nomenclature had better be after doing it himself."

But when Grey arrived and the situation was laid before him, the explanation was not at the moment forthcoming. He evaded it as deftly as he knew how, which, if the truth be told, was not by any means to the taste of either of the ladies. It would have been an easy matter to clear the mystery for Hope, but he hesitated to confess to Minna, in the presence of the others, that he had been sailing under false colours. She was a sensitive child, and serious, and he had no relish for inflicting the pain that his unmasking would, he knew, entail. So he simply said:

"Ah, that's a long story and we'll have it at another time. Just now I want to know what Miss Van Tuyl is going to wire to her doting father."

O'Hara excused himself and went out, and Miss von Altdorf extracted a novel from her satchel and buried herself in its pages.

"Wire him," Hope directed, "that I've gone on with you unexpectedly to Kürschdorf to secure rooms for the royal obsequies, and that he is to follow tomorrow night with the luggage."

"But he won't get it until late tonight, you know; possibly not until tomorrow morning," Grey told her.

"No, he won't get it until after two o'clock tomorrow, at the earliest," she replied, smiling.

"How do you know that?" he asked, surprised.

"Because he went to Trouville last night to see a man," she laughed. "He does not leave there until nine-one tomorrow morning, and it takes these crawling French railway trains five hours to make the journey."

XIII

"KÜRSCHDORF," THE guide-books will tell you, "is the Capital of the Kingdom of Budavia; 118 miles from Munich and forty-nine miles from Nuremberg. It stands on both banks of the Weisswasser, united by the Charlemagne and Wartberg bridges, 400 yards long. Surrounded by towering mountains its King's Residenz Schloss, erected 1607–1642, rises like the Acropolis above the dwellings and other buildings of the city. The steep sides of the Wartberg (1,834 feet) rise directly from amid the houses of the town, and it is on one extremity of the elevation that the imposing royal palace is located, with its 365 rooms, frescoes and statues, a 'Diana' of Canova, a 'Perseus' of Schwanhaler, a 'Sleeping Ariadne' of Thorwaldsen, and casts. The palace gardens are two miles long, and consist of a series of terraces overlooking the Wartberg valley on one side and a fertile plain on the other."

The guide-books, too, will tell you of the Königsbau, a quarter-mile long, containing a coffee house, the Bourse, and the Concert Hall; and of the Museum, where the chief treasures of Kürschdorf are on view daily (10 A. M. TO 4 P. M.); and of the Hof Theatre, and of the beer gardens. And they will give you a long and detailed description of the cathedral, completed in 1317, with its spire 452 feet high, ascended by 575 steps, its wonderful astronomical clock, and its great west window. They will even tell you that the best shops are in the Schloss Strasse, and that the Grand Hotel Königin Anna is a first-class and well-situated hostelry. But in no one of them will you find any mention of the most ancient dwelling house in all Kürschdorf, a quaint, dark stone building, on the Graf Strasse, only a stone's throw from the Friedrich Platz and two blocks away from the Wartburg Brücke.

At the moment Carey Grey was sending his telegram from the railway station at Château-Thierry to Nicholas Van Tuyl, in Paris, Count Hermann von Ritter, Chancellor of Budavia, was standing at a rear window of this venerable Kürschdorf mansion, gazing out upon a spacious and orderly rose garden. He was very tall and very angular. From a fringe of silver-white hair rose a shining pink crown; from beneath bushy brows of only slightly darker grey appeared small, keen black eyes; and a moustache of the same colour, heavy but close-cropped, accentuated rather than hid a straight, thin-lipped, nervous mouth. His head was bent thoughtfully forward and his hands, long and sinewy, with sharply defined knuckles, were clasped behind his back.

The drawing-room in which he stood was large and square, with high walls hung with many splendid pictures in heavy gilded frames. The furniture was massive and richly carved. Rococo cabinets held a wealth of curios—odd vases and drinking cups of repoussé work in gold and silver; idols from the Orient, peculiar antique knives—bodkins and poniards, and carvings of jade and ivory and ebony. The polished floor was strewn with Eastern rugs of silken texture, and at the doors and windows were hangings of still softer fabric and less florid colour and ornamentation.

After a little the Count crossed to a table on which stood lighted candelabra, and taking out his watch glanced at it with some show of impatience. Almost at the same moment a bell jangled, and very soon after a portière was raised by a servant wearing the Court mourning livery.

"Herr Captain Lindenwald, your Excellency!" he announced. And the Captain entered, saluting.

He was flushed and somewhat ill at ease, and the Chancellor's icy manner as he bade him be seated was not altogether reassuring.

"I am very much distressed over the news conveyed by your telegram," began the older man, when he had taken a chair at a little distance from his visitor. "Any delay at this juncture, you must understand, is only calculated to result in complications. Was His Royal Highness so violent that to bring him with you was impracticable?"

Lindenwald hesitated for just the shade of a second, his fingers playing nervously with the arm of his chair.

"I regarded the risk as too great," he ventured.

"That is no answer," the Count returned, irritably. "I asked you if he was violent."

"Yes, Count, he was," replied the Captain, with sudden assurance. "He was very violent at intervals. It would have been impossible to get him here without his causing a scene at some stage of the journey and probably revealing his identity. Besides, it was most dangerous. He was liable to evade his watchers and throw himself from the train."

The annoyance of the Chancellor increased.

"You have never heard, Captain," he said with a sneer, "that there are such things as handcuffs and strait-jackets."

"Ah, but Count," pleaded the other, in a tone of conciliation. "His Royal Highness! Could I put the Crown Prince to such humiliation? You know yourself that I would not be justified. It was better, it seemed to me, to have him safely confined in a private hospital in Paris for the present. In a little while, perhaps, his mind will clear."

"What is the form of his mania?"

"It is most peculiar," explained the Herr Captain. "You understand, of course, that until five months ago he had no idea whatever that he was who he is. He was, as you have been told, a valet, but a very superior man of his class. It is most certainly true that blood counts. He had all the inherent dignity of birth. His mind was far above his assumed station. All this you know. You may not have heard, though, that he was employed by an American stock broker named Grey who one day embezzled four hundred thousand marks and ran away."

"Yes," put in the Count, "I was informed of that as well."

"Just so. Well," continued the Captain, "His Royal Highness now, strangely enough, imagines that he is Grey."

"Imagines that he is an embezzler?" queried Ritter.

"Precisely. He even cabled to New York giving his Paris address, and the United States Embassy there was for arresting him and having him extradited."

"And when did this mania develop?"

"After the death of the Herr Doctor Schlippenbach."

The Chancellor sat thoughtfully rubbing together his long, virile hands.

"But I thought that this man Grey, this embezzler, committed suicide—was drowned or something."

"He was," Lindenwald assented, "at least he is supposed to be dead."

"It will be possible, I presume," the Count pursued, after another moment of meditation, "to have the present temporary regency continued by simply proving that Prince Maximilian, the heir apparent, is alive and mentally incapacitated, though to have had him here in the flesh would have been far better. And now as to these proofs—I am in possession of copies of the papers, but where are the originals?"

The Captain shifted uneasily in his chair, and his eyes refused to meet those of his interlocutor.

"That is a question, Count," he replied.

"A question!" cried the other, surprised and annoyed. "Why a question? Surely you are in possession of them!"

"Alas, I am not!"

His Excellency, his face crimson, sprang to his feet.

"My God, Captain!" he exclaimed in a rage, "you exasperate me beyond all bearing."

"I am deeply sorry, Count von Ritter," returned Lindenwald, "but if you will hear me for one moment you will know that I am not to blame."

"Excuses will not avail," he retorted, glowering. "You are a bungler, sir, a bungler. You have been either criminally careless in this matter or intentionally—yes, Captain, intentionally criminal."

"Your Excellency!" The Captain arose with a fine assumption of anger. "I permit no man, your Excellency——"

The Chancellor's lips were close pressed. His beady eyes were two points of fire.

"Tut, tut," he said, "this is neither the time nor place for that sort of thing. I am pained, distressed, mortified. From first to last your mission has been a series of blunders. Delay has followed delay; excuse has followed excuse; and now, at the crucial moment, comes the climax of your incapacity. A child could have done better. Knowing the importance of getting the Prince of Kronfeld here while His Majesty still lived you, on one pretext and another, dawdled away week after week in London and Paris; you permitted knowledge of the existence of the Prince to leak out; you could not even hide your stopping place from Hugo's emissaries—ah, you see I am well posted—and finally you come here not only without the heir but without the documents that are absolutely essential to the continuance of the direct succession."

Lindenwald listened, cowed and speechless. After a little, however, he spoke falteringly, while the Count, his hands behind him, strode excitedly up and down the large, square drawing-room.

"If you will but hear me," he protested, sullenly, "I think—I am indeed almost certain, your Excellency, that I can show you I am at least not altogether to blame. The Herr Doctor was ill when he landed in England. He was, moreover, most eccentric and most self-willed. And His Royal Highness was of the Herr Doctor's mind, always. For me to make a more expeditious journey was, under the circumstances, impossible. It appeared to me that it was the Herr Doctor's object to delay our arrival until after the death of His Majesty. Then, as you know, Herr Doctor Schlippenbach died, somewhat suddenly, and the madness of the Prince ensued."

"But the papers, the papers?" cried von Ritter, irritably, halting in his walk. "What of them?"

"The Herr Doctor never so much as showed them to me, Count. They were, I understand, in a strong-box, of which he and Prince Maximilian had duplicate keys. But the strong-box when we reached Paris was not brought to our hotel. Schlippenbach seemed to think it would be safer at the railway station. I argued with him, but to no avail. There was a fire, you remember, at our hotel in London, and that it and its contents were not destroyed was simply miraculous. It was that which frightened the Herr Doctor, and he refused to risk it in another hotel. Well, your Excellency, after his death we could find no trace of the box. The receipt for it had disappeared. I did my utmost to locate and secure it, but as yet I have been unsuccessful. I have tracers out, however, and it may be discovered any day."

"Bah!" almost shrieked the Chancellor, irascibly, "and a throne hangs on the slender thread of that 'may be.' Unless the box is found, Captain, it will be well for you to—but it is needless for me to suggest. You yourself know that your life, henceforth, would be not only useless, but a burden."

Lindenwald's chin dropped and his eyes sought the floor.

"The box shall be found," he said; but the assurance in his tone was meagre.

"And His Royal Highness," continued von Ritter, "is in a sanitarium in Paris?"

"Yes, Count; the sanitarium of——"

But a rap on the door cut short his answer, and the name either was not pronounced or was drowned in the Chancellor's stentorian:

"*Herein!*"

A footman handed His Excellency a telegram, and with a "Pardon me, Captain!" he opened it.

Years of diplomatic training had given the Count von Ritter a command of his facial muscles that was perfect. Not by so much even as the quiver of an eyelash did he signify the character of the tidings thus conveyed to him. Having read the message at a glance he refolded the paper with some deliberation, and then turning to Lindenwald again, asked:

"In whose sanitarium did you say?"

"Dr. De Cerveau's."

"You saw him there yourself?"

"Yes, Count."

"And there is no possible chance of his escaping?"

"None whatever, Count."

His Excellency took another turn to the window overlooking the rose garden, his head bowed meditatively. Lindenwald was still standing, his arm resting on the high back of the chair from which he had risen.

"You are quite sure," His Excellency pursued, when he was again opposite the Captain, "that we need have no apprehension on that score?"

"Quite sure, Count von Ritter."

Very slowly, and with a care and precision that emphasised the action, the Chancellor again unfolded the telegram he held and extended it towards Lindenwald.

"Then you will, perhaps, explain to me what that means?" he said, with a calmness that was portentous.

The face of the Herr Captain went ashen white. He caught his breath sharply, and his left hand gripped the chair back where a second before his arm had rested.

"*Am leaving this evening, Orient Express,*" he read. "*Have me met on arrival.* ARNDT."

He made as if to speak, but his lips emitted no sound.

"Well? Well?" queried the Count, impatiently. "What is it? Explain it. That is from His Royal Highness, isn't it?"

"I—I—you see, I—" stammered the Captain, dazed and affrighted, "I—I am not so sure. It may be a hoax—a trap."

Von Ritter's eyes poured out upon him their contempt.

"A hoax, a trap," he sneered. "No, no, unless it be a trap in which to catch a certain officer of the Army who is not so very far away. I think, Captain, that it is useless to prolong this interview," and he pressed an electric button in the table under his thumb.

Captain Lindenwald bowed, but said nothing.

At the same moment the footman reappeared and at a signal from the Chancellor lifted the portière, and the Captain went rather shamefacedly from the room.

When the Count heard the street door close he pressed the button in the table again, and to the footman who entered he said:

"Otto, I wish to speak to the Chief of Police. Call him up, and when you have him on the telephone let me know."

He walked to the window again. The moon had risen, and the rose garden was clad in luminous white with trimmings of purplish grey and black shadows.

XIV

PASSENGERS for Kürschdorf by the Orient Express change cars at Munich, which, if the train is on time, is reached at 12.24 on the day following the departure from Paris. On this particular Monday the express was nearly forty minutes late, and, as the connecting train was timed to start at 1.02, the transfer was of necessity accomplished with somewhat undignified expedition. That it was accomplished at all, however, and that the quartet, of which Carey Grey was one, was so fortunate as to secure a compartment to itself, were subjects for mutual congratulation.

The journey from the French to the Bavarian capital had been rife with explanations. To Hope Van Tuyl, Grey had made the entire situation most clear, though he considerately refrained from revealing any feature or incident that would tend to alarm her. In his interview with Minna von Altdorf he had brought to bear all the tact of which he was possessed. It was no easy matter for him, in view of his duplicity that day at Versailles, to make her a completely veracious statement of the facts; and it was especially difficult because of her veneration for her great-uncle, the late Herr Schlippenbach, whom Grey could not but regard as an egregious knave.

She had been startled, surprised, pained, and bewildered by turns as he told her the story, but she never once questioned the truth nor doubted the honesty of the narrator.

"I simply can't understand it," she said, with distress in her pathetic eyes. "Why should Great-uncle Schlippenbach do such a thing? Why should he? How could he?"

"And I am just as much in the dark as you are," Grey answered, soothingly. "I have thought it over continually, and I can't arrive at any satisfactory conclusion. I don't remember ever having seen him, and why he should have selected me for this great honour—for, after all, it is an honour to be elevated to the throne, isn't it?" he laughed—"I can't imagine."

"We always knew he was eccentric," the Fraülein went on. "He had most marvellous ideas on certain subjects, but I won't believe he was criminal. He must have been just a little bit insane."

And then Grey asked her how it came that she joined the little party in London.

"You see, Great-uncle Schlippenbach wrote me that he was going to Budavia and asked me if I would like to go with him and see my sister in Kürschdorf," she explained. "That was reasonable enough—there was nothing insane about that, was there? My school term had just ended, and it was a question whether I should make my home with my sister over here or return to America with him."

"And he told you I was your uncle?"

"Oh, yes. You know I have an uncle in New York. His name is Max Arndt. That is true. And he told me that you were he."

Grey shook his head in token of his perplexity.

"What became of your Great-uncle Schlippenbach's luggage?" he asked, suddenly, after a pause.

"I have it with me," the girl answered, frankly. "I shall take it to my sister's."

"Have you opened it?"

"No. I thought that she and I would open it together."

"It is possible, you know, that it may contain something that will give us a hint as to his motive in this matter," Grey said, in explanation of his interest.

"Oh, I do hope so," the Fräulein returned. "I am so anxious about it."

Grey was on the point of leaving the compartment, when he felt a hand holding the hem of his coat.

"I have just one question to ask," said the girl as he turned. She was not looking at him, but she still retained her hold.

"Well?" he queried, laconically; and his voice was kindly inviting.

"Would you mind very much if I—that is to say, may I, still, although you are not really, but—may I go on calling you

Uncle Max?" The hesitating embarrassment of the first part of her utterance was followed by a nervous blurting of the question in conclusion.

"I shall feel very much hurt, Minna," Grey answered, "if you call me anything else." And he took the little hand from his coat and pressed it affectionately.

* * * * *

When the train for Kürschdorf arrived at Anslingen, on the Budavian border, there was more than the ordinary delay. There was, moreover, evidence of something unusual in the throng upon the platform and the suppressed excitement of those composing it. Johann, who had sprung out instantly from the third-class carriage in which he and Marcelle were travelling—his object being to secure the passage of the party's luggage through the Custom House—was at once recognised and besieged by a horde of questioners.

"The Prince!" they cried with one accord. "You are with him, are you not? Where is he? In which carriage? What is he like?" And he had no little difficulty in shaking them off and attending to the business in hand.

By some mysterious means the report had spread, and what was at first mere rumour had later found substantial confirmation in the discovered presence at the station of two distinguished personages: General Roederer, Commander of the Budavian army, and Prince von Eisenthal, conservative leader of the Budavian Assembly; each accompanied by a more or less gorgeously uniformed retinue.

Grey, looking from the carriage window, noted the crowd with some little apprehension. He glanced at O'Hara and saw that he too suspected the cause. To the two ladies of the party nothing had been said of the telegram addressed to the name appended to the Lindenwald despatch, and they consequently saw less of significance in the demonstration, though they noted the gathering as extraordinary.

As Grey peered at the constantly increasing throng he wondered whether his message had been ill-considered. He had, in a way, sent it blindly, not knowing whether Ritter was an ally or a dupe of the conspirators, and he had sent it knowing that, in either event, Lindenwald was on the spot to take whatever ground he chose and to use whatever argument he deemed most fitting. If the Captain so fancied he could have him arrested on the charge of being a pretender to the throne, and would, armed with that strong-box left by old Schlippenbach, have small difficulty in proving his allegation. For exoneration he himself might appeal to his Government, but as an absconding defaulter he could look for meagre assistance from that quarter. O'Hara had told him it was dangerous business, but he had spurned advice, and now he was face to face with the consequences, whatever they might be. He was a trifle nervous, his heart was beating faster than its wont, and there was a red spot in each cheek; but even while looking on the darkest side of the picture he regretted nothing. This crisis had to be faced in one form or another, and he was glad the moment for facing it had arrived.

There was a movement in the crowd a few yards down the platform. The police were ordering the people back and clearing a lane beside the railway carriages. Grey thrust his head from the window and saw coming down this lane, in company with the train conductor, an army officer in olive green uniform and black helmet. Upon his breast was pinned a rosette of crepe, the insignia of mourning for the dead monarch.

At the door of each first-class compartment the two men halted for a second, asked a question and came on. But before they reached the carriage in which Grey was waiting, Johann, who had discerned their object, overtook them and led the way. Meanwhile, though Grey had not spoken, his companions had, intuitively, or by some other occult means, become aware of what was impending, and sat in breathless expectation.

And then, suddenly, before anticipation had been quite dethroned by realization, the officer was saluting, was being joined by his superiors and the rest of their retinues, and Grey was standing erect and dignified, listening to a little formal speech of welcome from the bearded lips of Prince von Eisenthal.

The crowd cheered lustily, of course, and cried: "God save Prince Max!" And a band played the Budavian national anthem. After which, or rather in the midst of which, the Prince and General Roederer entered the compartment with Grey and his friends, their suites finding places as best they could elsewhere, and the train, with much ringing of bells and blowing of whistles, moved off into the valley of the Weisswasser, its locomotive now gay with many Budavian flags and streamers of red and white bunting—colours of the royal house of Kronfeld.

Grey's relief from the tension of uncertainty found expression in an interested animation that impressed Prince von Eisenthal most favourably. He asked many questions concerning the affairs of the little kingdom, both political and commercial, and exhibited a concern over the conservative policy of the late King that was especially pleasing to the leader of the conservative forces. General Roederer, meanwhile, addressed himself to the ladies and Lieutenant O'Hara. He was a bluff but gallant old fellow, with ruddy complexion and iron-grey hair, and he possessed a quaint humour that kept the little company in gay spirits throughout the hour of the trip from the frontier to the capital.

"I am deeply regretful, your Royal Highness," he said to Grey, as the towers and spires of Kürschdorf came into view, "that we are not at liberty to offer you such a demonstration on your arrival as I should have liked. But His Majesty, the late King, you understand, is still above sod, the Court is in mourning, and the Prince Regent deemed it unfitting to give you more than the most informal of welcomes."

Grey bowed his acknowledgment.

"I am glad," he said, tactfully, "though I do not fail to appreciate the expression of good will in your desire. The Prince Regent's views and mine, in this matter, are in perfect accord."

But, however well the ideas of the supposed heir and the Prince Regent may have coincided, the populace was by no means of the same mind. It is not every day that a Prince of Kronfeld arrives in Kürschdorf—not every day that a new King comes from across the sea to take his place as ruler of his people—and the loyal townsfolk, despite the brevity of time between announcement and arrival, and the expressed opposition of their temporary ruler to anything in the nature of an ovation, hung gay banners amid the mourning drapery of their house fronts, closed their offices and shops and turned out in gala dress and mood to crowd the streets, the squares and the cafés.

As the train drew slowly into the railway station Grey leaned over and took Hope's hand.

"I'll probably have to leave you for a little," he said, regretfully, "but O'Hara will see that you get to the hotel, and I'll try to look in this evening."

Outside the station a landau, its panels decorated with the royal arms and drawn by six cream-white Arabian horses in glittering, gold-mounted harness, stood in waiting, with coachman, footman and postillions in the purple and scarlet livery of the Court; while thirty yards away, in line along the opposite side of the Bahnhof Platz, was a troop of the King's Cuirassiers, their breastplates and helmets of silver and gold glinting fiery red in the glow of the sunset.

Cheer after cheer rang out as Grey, with the Prince on his right and the General on his left, passed through the station, followed by the welcoming company that had escorted him from Anslingen, and took his place in the waiting carriage. And, as the little procession of which he was the dominating feature wound through the boulevards and streets of the new town and across the beautiful Charlemagne bridge over the turbulent Weisswasser into the more ancient and picturesque quarter of the city, the cheering, it seemed to him, grew louder and more continuous. At one point a group of young girls in white frocks and red ribbons ran out into the roadway to spread flowers in the path of his equipage, and at another a chorus of a hundred students, crowded on the balconies of a *Brauerei*, greeted his coming with a patriotic glee, sung as only male voices of Teutonic breeding and training can sing choruses.

Grey's emotions during this drive were novel and complex. There were moments when he almost felt that he was indeed the Prince—not that any marvellous transubstantiation had taken place, but that he had always been so—and that all this homage, this enthusiastic applause and adulation were his by right; and there were moments when his heart grew sick at the fraud, the imposition, the error, and he knit his brows and reproached himself for letting the deception go so far.

The magnitude the affair had suddenly assumed appalled him. Heretofore he had regarded it as a mere personal matter. He had been outraged, his honour sullied, his life threatened, and he was justified, he had told himself, in using every means within his power to bring his enemies to book. But he had not perceived the possibilities of permitting this line of investigation to run on unchecked. In a single moment the adventure had become a matter of national import. He was guilty now of masquerading as heir to the throne of a European monarchy. Hitherto the crime lay at the doors of a few conspirators, who, to serve certain nefarious ends of which he knew nothing, had striven to secure for him the crown. In that plot he had personally had no part. Everything had been done without his cognisance or consent; but now it was not they alone who were forcing the scheme to a consummation. He had, practically, for the time being at least, joined hands with them and was passively allowing their plans to be carried out, though fully aware of the impious character of the whole proceeding.

And the enormity of his thoughtless offence was at each foot of the way made more and more apparent by these cheering masses of people. When they should learn that they had been tricked, what explanation would serve to assuage their resentment? Love and homage would be turned to hatred and vengeance, and no excuse that he could offer would have any weight against their sense of outraged loyalty.

Then his thoughts took a new trend, and he asked himself how it was possible that old Schlippenbach and his fellow-plotters had been able thus to fool the conservative leaders of a great nation regarding a matter so vital to the very existence of their most cherished institutions as the legitimate succession to the regal sceptre. What incontrovertible proofs had it been possible to offer in order to bring about this ready acceptance of a man whom the Budavian people had never seen to rule over their nation's destinies? After all, there was where the blame must lie. The preposterousness of the proposition, it seemed to him, should have been apparent to the most simple-minded.

And, as he thought, the landau, with the flashing cuirassiers galloping ahead and behind and on either side, began the tortuous ascent of the Wartburg by the wide, wooded avenues that wind from the palace gates through the sumptuous royal gardens up to the imposing Residenz Schloss on the mountain's apex. Now and then, through rifts in the foliage, Grey got glimpses of the vast, formidable, castle-like pile of sombre stone perched far above him, the outline of its battlemented towers showing sharp and clear against the pink of the sunset-tinted sky; and it seemed to frown forbiddingly, resembling more a great fortress at this distance than the magnificent palace it is.

Twenty minutes later, to a musical fanfare of bugles, a clinking of bit chains and a rattle of steel-shod hoofs on stone paving, the carriage swept in under the great grey *porte-cochère*; the massive oaken doors of the Schloss swung impressively inward, and Chancellor von Ritter, in his robes of office, with a dozen attendants at his back, stood in token of formal welcome on the threshold.

To Grey's immense relief, however, the ensuing formalities were of the briefest description, and almost immediately he found himself proceeding under the Chancellor's guidance and direction toward a suite of rooms in the Flag Tower that had been prepared against his coming.

XV

THE Grand Hotel Königin Anna at Kürschdorf is much like the Schweitzerhof at Lucerne. It stretches its long, yellow front, bordered by a stone terrace, along the wide Schloss Strasse, on the other side of which, shaded by four rows of leafy linden trees, is the Königin Quai, skirting the fast-flowing Weisswasser. At one end of the Quai is the Wartburg Brücke, and at the other the Kursaal.

At about ten o'clock on the morning following his arrival in Kürschdorf, O'Hara appeared on the terrace with a troubled expression on his usually care-free face and a newspaper in his hand. The events of the previous evening had filled him with an apprehension greater even than that which had beset his friend. Being himself a subject of monarchical rule, and appreciating by reason of his breeding and environment the very serious nature of the affair, he viewed these late developments with less leniency than would naturally temper the consideration of a citizen of a republic, whose knowledge of the ethics of dynasties had been gleaned chiefly from books.

Grey, in allowing himself to be invested with royal honours, had cut loose from O'Hara's counsel. The Crown Prince was no longer travelling *incognito*. He was now within the very shadow of the throne that awaited him, and was consequently hedged in by all the formalities of the Court. Yesterday they were able to consult as man to man on an equal footing. Today a gulf divided them. It would be possible, of course, for O'Hara to present himself at the Palace and crave an audience, but it was doubtful whether anything approaching a private consultation could be managed. The American now, oddly enough, was not his own master. Otherwise he would have come to the hotel the evening before, as he had planned. He belonged to the state, and, if rumour spoke truly, he was, and had been since his arrival at the Residenz Schloss, under the strictest surveillance.

There was a hint of this in the paper that O'Hara carried, and the very air was pregnant with more or less detailed gossip, sensational in the extreme. At breakfast the Irishman had overheard a conversation at the next table to the effect that the Crown Prince was quite mad and had been locked in a dungeon under the Palace in the care of a half-dozen burly wardens. Everyone was talking on the same subject. An officer in uniform, connected with the Royal Horse Guards, was reported to have said that Prince Max had attempted suicide on his way from Paris, and O'Hara, knowing this to be untrue, discounted most of the other tales as equally baseless. Nevertheless, he was very considerably disturbed. He longed to act, but realised that his hands were tied. All that was left for him to do was to wait with what patience he could command until something further developed. And so he lighted a cigar and strolled forth across the Schlosse Strasse to the Quai, where, presently, he was joined by Miss Van Tuyl and the Fräulein von Altdorf.

They, too, had heard the rumours with which the very atmosphere was vibrant, and they came to him with long faces seeking reassurance.

"Isn't it possible to find out something definite?" Hope asked, plaintively. "Surely there must be some authority somewhere. You are his friend and you have a right to know. Why not go to see General Roederer? Let us get a carriage and we will all three go."

"I should be only too glad, Miss Van Tuyl," O'Hara replied, "if I thought anything was to be gained by it; but the truth of the matter is, you are unnecessarily alarmed. Carey is all right. Don't you pay any attention to these cock-and-bull stories. He has done this thing with his eyes open, and if we go interfering we may upset all his plans. We shall hear from him some time during the day, I feel certain. But if we don't I'll see that you have the facts before you sleep tonight. By the way, have you heard from your father?"

"Oh, yes. I had a telegram late last night. He is on his way. He will be here this evening."

"Good. Two heads are better than one, and when he arrives we'll find out what we want to know if we have to blow up the palace to do it. But I really feel that we shall have tidings from His Royal Highness before many hours." And he laughed in his characteristic rollicking fashion.

"It all seems just like a dream to me," said Minna, soberly. "I'm completely dazed. So much has happened in the last week that I hardly know what I'm doing. And now I shouldn't stop here another minute, for I'm sure my sister will be at the hotel and those stupid people will not know where to tell her to find me."

"We'll all go over and sit on the terrace," suggested O'Hara. "The band will be playing before long, and they tell me it is a very good one."

On the journey from Paris the Irishman and the Fräulein had been much in each other's company, and the growth of their mutual interest had been more than once remarked by both Grey and Miss Van Tuyl. Now, as he gazed at her fresh young beauty, there was a tenderness in his eyes, the meaning of which there was no mistaking. Hope saw it, and when the terrace was reached she excused herself and went inside, leaving them together.

"You will be going to your sister's today, then, I suppose," said the soldier, when they had found places under the shade of an awning not too close to the band stand and well away from the other loungers; in his tone was regret.

"Yes," Minna answered, and her accent, too, was regretful. "Her house is to be my home after this, you know."

"And there'll be somebody that will miss you very much," O'Hara ventured. His eyes had grown worshipful, and the girl's colour deepened as she looked into them.

"And I shall miss somebody very much," she returned, with a tincture of coquetry; adding, after a briefest moment, "Miss Van Tuyl is lovely. I feel as if I had known her always."

"But I wasn't speaking of her," he protested, softly. "She'll miss you, I dare say; but there's a man who'll miss you a whole lot more—miss you as he never thought it would be possible for him to miss anyone."

The girl's eyes drooped under the ardour of his gaze, and her cheeks flushed pinker still at his words. Her heart fluttered with an emotion that was new to it, and that she did not quite understand. She had experienced it once or twice before, in lesser degree, on the train when this big, hearty, boyish fellow had—not altogether by chance—touched her hand. It made her mute then, and now her tongue was again for the moment tied.

"But I am not going far," she replied, when utterance returned; "my sister's place is only a mile or two out of town, and the man has told me that he is very fond of walking."

"And may he come?" he pleaded, eagerly, his face suddenly alight with the smile she had grown to regard as not the least of his attractions. "May he?"

"Why not?" she asked, laughing lightly.

"Yes, why not?" he repeated, joyously. "Since he will want to see her very much, and since she has not denied him."

Frau Fahler, Minna's sister, was much older than she; a woman of thirty-four at least, short, stout and fair-haired, but with eyes of that deep pansy blue which was a family characteristic. She arrived about eleven o'clock in a rather quaint-looking country wagon, and she carried off the Fräulein almost immediately, in spite of the urging of Hope and O'Hara that she would stop for luncheon and delay the parting until afternoon.

Minna was naturally loth to leave until some tidings had been received from the Palace, but her sister had a dozen reasons for her haste, and so it was arranged that when towards evening her luggage was sent for, the messenger should be given whatever news had arrived.

Hope's anxiety meanwhile had grown with every passing minute. O'Hara's assurances were well intentioned, but, backed only by surmise, they were by no means satisfying.

"I don't suppose he can come himself, or he would be here," she said, in reply to his oft-repeated explanation that a Crown Prince is not wholly his own master, "but he certainly could send Johann or some one with a note."

But the afternoon wore away without any message. On the other hand, the rumours of the morning grew more ominous. A special session of the Budavian Assembly had been called for that very evening. A question, it was said, had arisen as to the legitimacy of the alleged heir apparent. Certain members of the Royal household were reported under arrest, charged with no less a crime than treason. The adherents of Prince Hugo were in the highest feather. Already the more optimistic were speaking of him as His Majesty. In the crowded cafés, the *Brauerei* and the beer gardens but the one subject was discussed; and the newspapers got out special extras, which hinted guardedly at the mystery, but gave absolutely no facts.

At seven o'clock Hope Van Tuyl drove to the railway station and met her father. She was nervously excited to the verge of hysteria, and Nicholas Van Tuyl had some difficulty in piecing together her somewhat disconnected and, it seemed to him at times, irrational statements. Eventually, however, by dint of careful questioning he became acquainted with the salient points of the situation; and later, at dinner, the Irishman supplied what was lacking in important detail.

"I agree with Lieutenant O'Hara," said Mr. Van Tuyl, in a tone that smacked of the judicial; "it is a very delicate problem, and one that must be handled with the utmost care. At the same time, my dear child, your anxiety is natural, and, though I think you have exaggerated the seriousness of the affair, I can well understand your impatience for facts. And facts we are going to have."

He smiled confidently, and his daughter's face brightened on the instant.

"All the time you have been telling me your story," he went on, "I have been trying to think of the name of a man I met in Munich a few years ago. He holds some high position here, and would be just the chap to help us now. We were excellent friends, and when we parted he begged me to come to Kürschdorf and visit him. Strange I can't think of his name."

"What about the American Minister?" O'Hara suggested.

"I doubt that he would know. Besides, under the circumstances, there's no use taking chances. If we told him the truth it would be a case of out of the frying-pan into the fire. Grey is extraditable, you know. I wonder if we could learn anything by attending this Parliament meeting?"

"We couldn't get in. I thought of that at once and made inquiries. It's an executive session."

Van Tuyl was silent for a minute or more, evidently deep in thought.

"I don't suppose you know the names of the high monkey-monks here, do you?" he asked, presently.

"I know a few," O'Hara answered. "There's Prince von Eisenthal, and Herr Marscheim, and Count von Ritter, and——"

"Aha!" cried the New York man, gleefully, "now you've hit it. Von Ritter—Count von Ritter. He is my Munich friend. What is he? What position does he hold?"

"He is what they call Chancellor, I believe; but in reality he's a sort of Prime Minister."

"That's our man, by all that's good!" Van Tuyl exclaimed. "We'll find where he hangs out and call on him. And, girlie," he added, turning to his daughter, "you'll know all about it in a few hours."

"He'll be at the Assembly session, of course," said O'Hara.

"Certainly. We'll go there and send him in a message, and I'll bet ten dollars to a cent he'll come a-running. He owes me a debt of gratitude; I put him in the way of placing a government loan at very good figures when the Budavian credit wasn't the best in all Europe by any means."

Hope smiled her gratitude. She had great faith in her father. He was of the type of successful Americans that do things.

XVI

THE apartment in the Flag Tower to which Carey Grey was conducted by Chancellor von Ritter was at the top of two flights of winding stone stairs, and the barred windows of its four rooms commanded a view of varied and picturesque loveliness. In the foreground were the Palace gardens, with their series of descending terraces, their fountains and statuary, their parterres of gay flowers, their gracefully curving driveways and gravelled walks, and their wonderful old trees of every shade of green leafage. Beyond the gardens were the red and grey roofs, the spires and steeples and domes and turrets of the city, divided by the sparkling silver-white waters of the rushing river, and beyond these stretched the fertile valley checkered with fields of ripening grain—yellow and orange and russet—and olive patches of woodland, and dotted with farm houses and cottages and barns and hayricks.

The rooms, themselves, were somewhat sombre. There was a small library, panelled and finished in black oak; a *salon*, long and high, with much tarnished gilt ornamentation and red upholstery; a tiny bare dressing-room, and a bedchamber with a great canopied bedstead, beside which stood a quaintly carved *prie-dieu*.

"Your Royal Highness will, I trust, be comfortable here," said the Chancellor, when he had walked with Grey from one room to another and the two were standing together in the long *salon*.

The American hesitated a moment before replying. He was revolving mentally several alternatives of action. It was his duty, he knew, not to let this farce proceed further; and yet he had thus far learned absolutely nothing.

"I shall," he said, at length, "be quite comfortable."

"If there is anything your Royal Highness desires," continued the Chancellor, "you have but to make it known."

The invitation arrested the whirl of indecision and settled the course of procedure.

"If you will be so good as to answer me a few questions, Count," Grey began, "I shall be indebted. Won't you sit down?"

Count von Ritter found a place for his angular length upon a settee beside a pedestalled bust of King Oswald the First, and Grey sank into a chair near by.

"I am entirely at your Royal Highness's disposal," the Chancellor avowed, amiably; and the American, not without some trepidation, it must be confessed, began:

"You understand, of course, that events in my career have followed one another in the most rapid succession during the past few months; and regarding some of the most important details I am entirely uninformed. You will be surprised, perhaps, to learn, for instance, that I do not know with any degree of definiteness how my identity was established. Herr Schlippenbach was my discoverer, of course, but with whom did he consult here and by what means was it made clear that I am really the abducted heir of the Budavian crown?"

Count von Ritter listened to the question with growing suspicion. Here were, perhaps, the first indications of that insanity of which Lindenwald had spoken.

"It does seem hardly possible, your Royal Highness," he replied, "that on such a vital matter you should have been left in ignorance. It was, I think, nearly a year ago that the first communication from the Herr Doctor Schlippenbach was brought to me by Herr Professor Trent."

"And who is Herr Professor Trent?" Grey asked, quickly.

"The Herr Professor," answered the Chancellor, "is the head of the University of Kürschdorf."

"And his reputation is, of course, beyond reproach, eh?"

"Quite beyond reproach, your Royal Highness."

"And what steps followed?" Grey pursued, inquisitorially, crossing his legs and leaning back in his chair.

"I took up the matter personally," the Count responded, with frankness. "I entered into correspondence with Schlippenbach at once, and after some months of writing back and forth he placed before me a very circumstantial story, which he afterward confirmed with documentary evidence—old letters, photographs, affidavits."

"And then?"

"When I had thoroughly assured myself of the authenticity of all he claimed, I brought the subject to the attention of the Privy Council, and eventually it was laid before His Majesty. In the meantime the Budavian Minister at Washington had been investigating, and the Budavian Consul at New York as well. But all that, of course, you know."

Grey nodded, dissembling. He was studying Count von Ritter as he spoke; noting every accent, every inflection, every expression, in an endeavour to decide whether he were innocent or guilty. Thus far he had been inclined to regard him as honest. It hardly seemed possible that one occupying his position could stoop to such chicanery. And the head of the university appeared likewise as too impregnably placed to be open to suspicion. The Budavian Minister and the Budavian Consul, however, he concluded could not be guiltless.

"And how did Captain Lindenwald chance to be chosen to meet me on my arrival in England?" he asked.

"Captain Lindenwald," answered the Chancellor, "is an officer of the Royal household—he was the late King's equerry—and he is, moreover, the brother of our Minister to the United States."

Grey smiled in spite of himself. Of Lindenwald's complicity he had had no doubt from the first. The fact that the Budavian Minister at Washington was his brother made it all the more probable that that dignitary was also criminally involved.

"Now, just one more matter, Count," the American continued. "Can you tell me anything of this Baron von Einhard?"

The Chancellor shrugged his square shoulders.

"The Baron is a supporter of Prince Hugo," he answered.

"That much I know," Grey returned. "And in his loyalty to his leader he is apt to be unscrupulous to the Prince's opponents?"

Count von Ritter smiled a trifle cynically.

"I have been led to understand so," he answered.

"He would pay well, I suppose, to get Prince Max out of the way just at this juncture? Is it not so?"

"The price asked would probably not deter him."

"And Captain Lindenwald—But no, of course not. It is silly of me to suggest such a possibility. You are satisfied of that officer's fealty, I am sure?"

The Chancellor straightened in his seat and leaned forward with an exhibition of concern that had hitherto been lacking.

"You do not make yourself altogether clear, your Royal Highness," he ventured. "Am I to understand that you have reason to suspect that Captain Lindenwald and the Baron von Einhard are——"

"Pardon me," interrupted Grey, pleased nevertheless at the awakened interest of the Chancellor, "I did not say so. I merely asked a question. You are satisfied of Captain Lindenwald's entire honesty and loyalty, are you not?"

"The Captain," von Ritter replied, guardedly, "has not been as eager as I could have wished at times, but I have never regarded him as venal."

"Then his explanation of why he left me in Paris, without so much as a word as to his going, and why that night an attempt was made to abduct me by persons in the employ of Baron von Einhard—I suppose he has made such an explanation—was entirely satisfactory to you?"

Grey sprung the question suddenly and noted scrutinisingly the effect.

The Chancellor's usually immobile features gave perceptible token of his surprise. His bushy brows raised the merest trifle, and his keen black eyes widened.

"His story was, I must confess, not altogether satisfactory, your Royal Highness," he answered, quietly; "it was, I may say, lacking in detail."

"I would suggest," continued Grey, in a tone equally repressed, "that you question him in the line I have indicated."

The Chancellor bowed.

"I have to thank you," he said, gravely. "I shall do so. That is very certain."

Grey arose and Count von Ritter got to his feet instantly. The American stood for a moment in indecision, very tall, very erect. There was no denying that he looked every inch the Prince. Whether to declare that he was not he hurriedly debated. Meanwhile the Chancellor was still striving to detect the madness of which Lindenwald had spoken. To each question he had given the most searching mental scrutiny; to each gesture, to each intonation he had paid the closest heed, but he had discovered practically no indication of the malady charged. With Grey's next utterance, however, all the fabric of his assurance fell crumbling.

"Count von Ritter," he said—he had been for a moment gazing out through the window at the varied landscape now dimming with the dusk, but as he spoke he turned and faced the Chancellor—"Count von Ritter, I can delay no longer in confiding to you a matter so grave that I scarcely know how to frame it in words. May I ask you to again be seated?" And he waved his hand towards the settee from which the Count had risen.

The Chancellor seated himself without speaking, and Grey resumed his place in the chair near him.

"The reason I have asked you what I have," continued he, speaking slowly and with more than his usual deliberation, "is that I have been—I was about to say astounded, but that is too weak a word—I have been stunned and dumfounded by the proved credulity of a nation which has the reputation, next to Russia, of possessing the most astute diplomats in all Europe. That a government so fortified could be tricked into placing its sceptre in the hands of an American citizen, whose ancestry shows no trace of Budavian blood and whose antecedents are an open book, seems out of all reason; and yet it is precisely what you and your confrères, Count, have, as is now conclusively evidenced, been led into."

Upon the Chancellor's face was an expression which Grey could not fathom. He was neither startled nor incensed. There was, indeed, just the faintest suspicion of amusement in his keen black eyes, mingled with a spirit of kindly indulgence.

"You mean," he said, quietly, "that you are not the heir?"

"Most assuredly," Grey answered, in amazement at his companion's inscrutable manner, "I am no more the Prince of Kronfeld than I am the Prince of Wales. I am Carey Grey, of New York, an American born and bred, who was drugged, hypnotised, mesmerised or what you please; made unknowingly to commit a theft, made unknowingly to cross the Atlantic, to travel under a false name, to attempt to usurp a title and a throne."

Count von Ritter's foot tapped the floor nervously. He laced his long, knotted fingers and unlaced them again.

"This is a very grave matter," he said, his voice low and steady, "and I shall lose no time in looking into it. As you say, such a thing would appear beyond the bounds of reason. Your Royal High—I beg your pardon! Mr. Grey, did I understand?" And there was a humouring leniency, not to say pity, in his tone—"you can imagine how much this statement of yours at this late hour will involve in the way of complications."

"That you were not enlightened earlier, Count," Grey continued, "was due to my desire to learn just how far the conspiracy had been carried. As a matter of fact, until I reached Anslingen this afternoon I had no positive assurance that the affair had gone further than Herr Schlippenbach and Captain Lindenwald. Of their intentions I was well satisfied, but concerning the chances for the ultimate success of their plans I was in the dark."

Again the two men stood up.

"And now," said the Chancellor, "as to dinner. A state banquet has been prepared at which your—pardon me!—at which *His* Royal Highness was to have presided. Under the circumstances, however, I presume you would prefer not to attend. If I may be permitted," he added, tactfully, "I will explain that His Royal Highness is indisposed."

"Thank you," Grey acquiesced, cheerily; "that's the better course—the only course, in fact. Unless you can yourself join me—and I suppose that is impossible—I'll dine alone here. And afterward I should like a conveyance to the Hotel Königin Anna. I have some friends there that I must see this evening."

The Chancellor bowed. The next moment he was gone, and Grey crossed to the open window and stood for a long while lost in thought. Meanwhile the gloom deepened over the valley and the room behind him grew dark.

He was awakened from his reverie by a rapping on the door, and in response to his permission to enter Johann came in, followed by porters with his luggage. Then the candles were lighted, and a little later his dinner was served.

Afterward he got into his evening clothes, and when he was quite ready he sent Johann to see if the carriage he had ordered was in waiting. But the boy returned with dismay mantling his usually placid features.

"The carriage is not coming, your Royal Highness," he said, with an accent of apology, as though the fault was his.

"Not coming?" Grey repeated in astonishment. "Why is it not coming?"

"None has been ordered, your Royal Highness."

"Then order one at once."

"I tried to, your Royal Highness; but I was not permitted."

Grey's customary calmness gave way to palpable irritation.

"What the devil do you mean?" he asked. "Am I a prisoner here?"

Johann's distress increased.

"It is not I, your Royal Highness, on whom the blame lies. Outside this door is a guard. He will not let me pass. He will not let your Royal Highness pass. He has orders."

The American strode angrily towards the door.

"We will see," he said, determinedly.

Outside a soldier was standing.

"What does this mean?" he asked, in as repressed a tone as he could muster. "Why will you not let my man do as I bid him?"

The sentry saluted respectfully.

"I have been ordered by my commanding officer, your Royal Highness," he answered.

"Ordered to what?" cried Grey.

"Ordered, your Royal Highness, to permit no one to leave the Flag Tower."

And he saluted again.

XVII

THE realisation that he was a prisoner aroused in Carey Grey a spirit of revolt. He thought that he had calculated the cost. He had foreseen that his confession would bring about complications, and had counted on perhaps a long and trying investigation, but he had not imagined that he would be deprived of his liberty pending the question's settlement. The fact that he had been honest should of itself, he argued, have entitled him to consideration; but his frankness had been misjudged and his candour rewarded with punishment.

Smarting under the indignity, he wrote a witheringly sarcastic note to Count von Ritter, and demanded that the guard should see to its expeditious delivery. At the end of an hour he received a brief reply:

"The Chancellor," it read, "regrets deeply that he is unable to aid Mr. Grey. The Chancellor repeated his interview of the early evening to His Highness, the Prince Regent, and it is by His Highness's command that the present temporary restraint exists."

Thereupon Grey set about devising some means of escape; but the barred windows and the armed guard, which, he learned from Johann, was not alone at his door but on the landings above and below and surrounding the Tower as well, were seemingly insurmountable obstacles. He thought of bribery, and as an entering wedge endeavoured to have a note taken to Miss Van Tuyl, offering a sum of money out of all proportion to the service, but the offer was phlegmatically declined.

It was very late before he threw himself upon the great high bed in the dingy bedchamber and tried to snatch a few hours' sleep; and he was up again at dawn. But if his slumber had been brief, Johann's had even been briefer. He had spent hours in conversation with the soldier in the passage, and he had gathered at least one fact of interest, if not of importance—there were other prisoners on the floor above. How many, he was unable to learn, and of the strength of the guard he was also uninformed. There would be a change, though, at seven o'clock, and then it would be possible to ascertain.

From the window of the library which was over the Tower door the approach of the relief and the departure of the night watch could be seen. The bars were too close to permit of a head being thrust between them, but the barracks were at some distance from the Palace, and the route, Johann said, lay diagonally across the uppermost terrace in full view of this particular window. There Grey watched, and promptly at seven, as the bell in the Bell Tower on another corner of the quadrangle clanged the hour, a cornet sounded and seven armed infantry men came marching over the stone pavement. That, he concluded, meant one man on each of the three landings and four men on guard below. Not counting the guard on the floor above, there were six against two, and escape under these conditions appeared hopeless. If, however, the prisoners on the floor above could be communicated with and a plan of concerted action agreed upon there might be a fighting chance of success. But the question was, how to reach them. The ceilings were high and the floors thick, and to invent and execute a code of signals by rapping would be a tedious and not at all promising undertaking. Nevertheless Grey was more than half inclined to try it. By piling one piece of furniture on another the ceiling could be reached readily enough, and by giving each letter of the alphabet its number it would be possible to hammer out words. Those above might not be able to hear or, hearing, might not be clever enough to understand, but the American was desperate, and, notwithstanding the odds against him, he determined after some little consideration to make the effort.

Upon a large table in the centre of the *salon* he and Johann lifted a smaller one which they brought from the library, and upon this in turn they placed a chair. To the top of this edifice Grey climbed, armed with a heavy walking-stick, with which he began a series of regular and irregular blows upon the heavy oaken panelling which ceiled the room. Having continued this for something like three minutes without intermission, he paused in the hope of some response. But none was forthcoming, and he repeated the signalling with increased vigour. When he halted again there was a distinct reply—an exact reproduction, in fact, of his rhythm—and the serious, anxious expression he had worn gave way to one of relief, if not indeed of triumph.

His next move was to repeat in strokes the entire alphabet, beginning with one for A, two for B, and so on. This was a long and rather laborious operation, but when he had finished he was given the prompt gratification of an alert understanding from those above, for immediately taking the cue, the answering thuds spelled out the word "window," and turning his glance in the direction of the barred casement he saw hanging there, at the end of an improvised string made of torn and tied strips of linen, a fluttering piece of paper.

With a single bound he reached the floor, and the next instant he was reading with eager interest the pencilled words:

"Write what you wish to say, attach it, pull gently twice, and we will raise it."

"Johann," he cried, enthusiastically, "see this! If those fellows have as much nerve as they have wit we'll soon be out of here, all right."

And while Johann read and smiled his approval Grey sat down and wrote.

For an hour or more questions and answers, propositions and suggestions, went back and forth from floor to floor by means of this novel line of communication, and by the end of that time a complete scheme of escape with all its details had been arranged and was mutually understood.

There were two prisoners above—a gentleman and his man; just as there were two prisoners below—a gentleman and his man. Who the two gentlemen were was not asked by either. That they were guarded in the Flag Tower was proof that their offences were political merely. Nevertheless, the two gentlemen resented the indignity put upon them, and both were anxious to escape. The two men were loyal to their masters and could be depended upon to act with valour. The gentleman above was unarmed, but the gentleman below had a revolver. The time agreed upon for the delivery was two o'clock in the morning. As that hour sounded from the Bell Tower the guards on their respective floors were to be called in on some pretext, overpowered and stripped of their uniforms, which would be donned by the two gentlemen. Their weapons would be appropriated, likewise, and thus disguised and armed it would be comparatively easy to make captive the guard on the first landing. There would then remain but the four soldiers outside the Tower, and the chances of their subduing were largely in favour of the prisoners, three of whom would by this time be as well equipped as the watch, while the fourth would have Grey's revolver. The advantage is invariably with the surprising party, and the plan was to take the guardsmen unawares and effect their capture before they were even conscious of attack.

All this having been definitely decided on there was nothing to do but wait, and the hours, for Grey at least, dragged interminably. Again and again at intervals he rehearsed the plan with Johann, so that there could be no possible chance of error, but this after a while grew monotonous and he looked about for something interesting to read. The books he found in the library, however, were not diverting. They were for the most part historical and written in the heaviest of German; nevertheless their very ponderousness was in a way an advantage. They provoked somnolence, and late in the afternoon the uninterested reader fell asleep and was so snugly wrapped in slumber when his dinner was brought in that Johann found it a rather difficult task to rouse him. He had slept but little the night before, and his rest on the train the night previous to that had been broken and fitful. His nerves needed just this repose, and when he finally awakened it was with a clearer eye and a steadier hand. He ate heartily of the distinctively Teutonic dishes that were provided, and when he finished he remarked to Johann on his general fitness, indulging in an Americanism which the valet vainly tried to interpret.

"I feel tonight, Johann," he said, stretching himself with arms extended and fists doubled, "that I could lick my weight in wildcats and paint whole townships red."

As the hours wore away he sat with one leg thrown over the arm of his chair, smoking placidly and with evident enjoyment. It was not until some time after the Bell Tower had bellowed its single note that Grey alluded to the business of the night.

"Everything is ready, is it, Johann?" he asked; "where are the thongs you made from the sheet?"

"Safe in my coat pockets, your Highness," the youth answered.

"Now you may bring me my revolver," the American continued; "it is on the cheffonier in my dressing-room."

The revolver was brought, and Grey examined its chambers once again to make sure that it was fully loaded. Then, throwing the end of his cigar through an open window, he lighted a cigarette and continued in desultory talk with his valet.

A few minutes before two he rose and went into his dressing-room, which separated the *salon* from the bedchamber. In the latter candles were alight, but the dressing-room was in darkness. He stepped behind the curtains, close to the wall, and stood there, silent, hidden, and shortly from the Bell Tower solemnly sounded the hour. Simultaneously Johann tried the door which gave from the little library on to the landing. But it was locked and bolted from without. Then he hammered loudly, a little excitedly; and very promptly the bolt was drawn and the key turned.

"Quick!" he cried to the guard, who swung open the heavy oaken planking. "Quick! His Royal Highness is ill! I fear that he is dying! Come!" And he started off hurriedly, the soldier following unsuspectingly.

In a second the little comedy was played. At the entrance to the dressing-room Johann stepped back and the guardsman went in ahead, to find his arms caught in a flash from behind by Grey and held hard and fast in spite of his struggles, while Johann slung about his wrists the heavy linen thongs and knotted them with deft and muscular hands. Meanwhile the fellow was kicking and stamping viciously, but, barring a barked shin for Johann and a bruised toe for Grey, the effects were not material. And, once his arms were bound and the glittering barrel of the revolver brought to his attention, his rebellion ceased. Then Johann bound his feet as well, having first marched him into the bedchamber and compelled him, protesting, to stretch himself upon the high, old-fashioned bed.

Grey was in the act of unbuckling the captive's belt when a pistol shot, muffled but unmistakable, echoed from overhead, and he stopped, breathless, just as a hoarse shriek split the silence which for an instant followed the report. The door from the library to the landing had been left open, and from that direction now came a scuffle of feet on stone, mingled with a succession of crashing, thumping, jolting noises, alarmed shouts and angry imprecations.

Through the three connecting rooms Grey dashed, revolver in hand and with Johann close at his heels. The lantern the guard had left on the landing had been knocked over and was out, but by the light from the open doorway they at once discovered the huddled, distorted body of a man, whose groans added to the bedlam of hurrying feet and excited voices from below and oaths, cries, and sounds of struggle from above.

And as they looked there came bounding down the stairs, by jumps of a half-dozen or more steps at a time, another figure, followed by futile shot after shot from rapidly belching revolver and rifle. The fugitive's feet landed on the groaning, doubled heap on the landing, and that he did not stumble to his death was a miracle. But he kept his balance, flashed by down the next winding flight, and, striking the first of the ascending guards, toppled him backwards against his followers.

For the space of a heart-beat Grey and Johann paused, staring at each other. In that instant of his passing both had recognised the fleeing prisoner. It was Captain Lindenwald.

And then, as they stood inert, the guard from above, his rifle still smoking, reached the landing, tripped over the crumpled body and went staggering, lurching, clutching at the air, towards the confusion below.

The moment for action had now come; and Grey, calm and collected in spite of the flurry of events, motioning to Johann to follow, ran swiftly down the stone stairs, which, once they were out of the meagre glow from the library, grew dark as Erebus. The struggling, swearing, wriggling mass blocked the way at the next landing, but Grey and the lad, guided by the sounds, were not taken unawares. They were, moreover, for the moment on their feet, which no one of the others was; and though they were caught by desperate hands and more than once dragged to their knees, their clothing torn and ripped, their hands scratched, and their arms and legs wellnigh disjointed, they kept their wits and gained the last flight of steps without serious injury.

Down this they veritably hurled themselves, and with no further impediment to delay them reached the open door of the Tower and dashed out onto the stone flagging of the upper terrace, into the brilliant starlight of the early morning.

"So far, so good," said Grey, inhaling deeply of the cool, clear air; and catching Johann's sleeve he pulled him back into the shadow of the buttress. "But," he added, "we are not free yet, are we? The gates of the Palace Gardens are locked at night, I suppose."

"Yes, your Royal Highness," the youth answered.

"Never mind that Royal Highness business now, Johann," he directed; "Herr Arndt will do for the present. I'm no more a Royal Highness than you are."

"Yes, Herr Arndt," acquiesced Johann, imperturbably, without change of tone, "and the walls are very high."

"Nevertheless, we had better move on in the direction of some exit," Grey advised, in a whisper; "it won't do to stop here. They may come rushing down on us at any minute. You know the way; you lead."

Johann started off to the right, hugging the Tower walls, and Grey followed. At a distance of fifty yards they came to a clump of shrubbery, into which the younger man plunged with Grey still close behind. Through this a gravelled path led into a wood, under the trees of which they walked in silence for at least a quarter of an hour, their course one of gradual descent.

"Without our hats we'll be suspicious figures in the streets of Kürschdorf," Grey observed, despondently, as they came out upon a driveway, "and our recapture is certain. After all, I don't see that we have gained a very great deal. The gates won't be open till morning, and by that time, if we are not captured inside, every exit will be guarded against us. Are the walls too high to scale?"

"Yes, Herr Arndt," answered Johann, respectfully, but he did not slacken his pace.

"What do you propose, then? Come, now, this is serious. You know every inch of ground here, don't you? Is there no way we can get out?"

"Yes, Herr Arndt," came the stereotyped answer.

"There is? Then why didn't you say so? How? In God's name, Johann, how?"

The youth halted and turned.

"At the head gardener's is a long ladder," he answered; "we are going to the head gardener's, Herr Arndt."

At the head gardener's they very shortly arrived. Johann's familiarity with the place was now more than ever evident. Without hesitation he entered one of the larger greenhouses, the door of which stood invitingly ajar, and, though it was quite dark within, he very promptly laid his hand upon a ladder which lay stretched against the wall to the right of the entrance. Having thus assured himself that it was in its usual place, he groped to the left and from a row of pegs there secured two hats; one of green felt and the other of dark straw, soiled and dilapidated, it is true, but in the present strait of the fugitives of inestimable value.

The high wall of the garden was, it subsequently developed, but a stone's throw distant, and the work of carrying and placing the ladder, climbing to the coping and springing over onto the border of soft turf without was a matter of a very few minutes.

"And now," said Grey, as with the faded and stained green hat upon his head he stood looking up and down the dark, silent street, "where are we to go? Our presence at a hotel would simply invite detection. It is too early for me to call on the American Minister. All of your usual haunts will be searched before sunrise."

"The sister of the Fräulein von Altdorf," suggested Johann, "to whom the Fräulein herself was going, lives in the country, about two miles away."

"You know where?" cried Grey, delightedly; "you can find it?"

"I know it well," answered the youth; "at the next farm I was born, Herr Arndt."

"Then we will go there, by all means."

And they set off walking rapidly through the narrow side streets of the old town to the bridge of Charlemagne, and thence across the river, and on through the wider avenue of the new city out into the silent lanes of the sweet-scented suburbs.

Both were busy with their thoughts and neither was inclined to conversation. After twenty minutes' trudging, however, Grey asked:

"Do you suppose that fellow on the landing will die, Johann?"

"That fellow?" repeated the valet, "which, Herr Arndt? Do you mean Lutz?"

"Lutz!" exclaimed Grey, surprisedly, "was Lutz there?"

"Of a certainty, Herr Arndt. Did you not see his face? It was Lutz who lay outside our door."

XVIII

THE rumoured meeting of the Budavian Assembly proved, like many other rumoured events, to be a canard, the only foundation for which was a hastily called session of the Privy Council. Before this august body, over which the Prince Regent presided, Chancellor von Ritter laid all the facts that had come into his possession; and very startling facts they were, including a confiscated letter from Baron von Einhard addressed to Captain Lindenwald, telling of the failure of the abduction plot and of the securing of that precious heirloom, the signet ring of the Prince of Kronfeld.

This communication gave indubitable proof that Lindenwald had been false to his trust, and it fully justified the Chancellor in having him placed under arrest. It did not tend, however, to throw any light on the mystifying main question. Was the man who had been welcomed with such acclaim on the previous evening really the Crown Prince, as every bit of evidence up to the time of his arrival tended to prove, or was he, as he claimed, simply the cat's-paw of a company of conscienceless conspirators?

The von Einhard letter would in a way indicate that his title was clear and genuine, as, had it been otherwise, there would have been no necessity to conspire with Lindenwald to bring about his abduction. Yet, if Lindenwald knew him to be the Crown Prince, why should he run the risk of dickering with the Baron, seeing that greater good fortune than he could possibly hope to earn by such a course lay in the direction of his faithful carrying out of his mission?

Upon these points the Privy Council debated long and eagerly, if not altogether wisely. Men are slow to confess even to themselves that they have been imposed upon, and the State Council had months before by an overwhelming majority declared its faith in the integrity of the claimant. It was, therefore, no more than to be expected that the majority should still favour the theory that Prince Max, in his assertion that he was simply a plain American citizen, was labouring under an hallucination. There had been a strain of dementia in the ruling line for seven generations, and this exhibition of mental malady was to those who now recalled the fact but another evidence of legitimacy.

On the minority who were known to be partial to Prince Hugo the proof of von Einhard's treachery served as an effective gag. They could not afford to imply sympathy for such conduct by opposition to the ruling notion; and so it happened that, while every phase of the question was discussed with much earnestness, there was ever an underlying sentiment that promised but one conclusion—the unqualified endorsement of the fancied unfortunately demented young Prince in the Flag Tower.

As the session was approaching its close, a card was brought to Count von Ritter. The Chancellor, however, deeply interested in the speech of the Secretary for Foreign Affairs, which was then in progress, laid it on the table before him without adjusting his glasses to read it, and had it not been for the dullness of the speech of the Secretary of War which followed, the session would probably have come to a vote and adjourned before he gave it heed. But as it chanced, bored by the prosiness of the speaker, he took up the piece of pasteboard, placed his *pince-nez* on the bridge of his nose, and read the name: "Mr. Nicholas Van Tuyl," with a pencil scrawl beneath: "Your friend of Munich and the Monterossan War Loan." Whereupon he arose instantly and tip-toed from the Council Hall into the ante-room adjoining, where Van Tuyl and O'Hara were with some impatience waiting.

Their reception by Count von Ritter was cordial in the extreme. The sentiment of the Council had served to lift a load from his shoulders, and he was in fine good humour.

"Remember you!" he cried, wringing Van Tuyl's hand, his small eyes alight, "of course I remember you; and my debt to you, too—Budavia's debt to you. Why, my dear sir, you should have had a decoration. The late King was very remiss in not sending you one. But we will do what we can to make up for it."

"Ah," returned the New York banker, "you are very good indeed, Count, and I am going to hold you to your word. Lieutenant O'Hara and I have come for something this evening—something we want very much, and something I feel sure you can give us."

The Chancellor bowed and stretched forth his hands with palms upturned and open, in signal of his willingness to give.

"What we desire," continued Nicholas Van Tuyl, smiling his recognition, "is information. There are many sensational reports abroad, as you probably know; but we men of finance are in the habit of discounting unverified rumours. We are not credulous. We want facts with an authority to back them up. We want confirmation or denial."

Von Ritter's geniality was still fervent.

"You wish to know, for instance—" he invited.

"We wish to know, Count, whether there is any basis for the story that His Royal Highness, Prince Maximilian, is being restrained of his liberty."

The Chancellor smiled a little patronisingly.

"Do they say that?" he asked.

"That is the least they say," Van Tuyl returned.

For a moment Count von Ritter hesitated.

"May I, without discourtesy, inquire why you are interested?" he questioned.

"We are interested," answered the New Yorker, promptly, "because he is our personal friend. I have known him for years, and Lieutenant O'Hara here has been with him, he tells me, continually from the day he left America."

The three were still standing; but now the Chancellor motioned his visitors to be seated.

"You in turn interest me," he said, as he took a chair and sat down facing them. "How long, Mr. Van Tuyl, have you known him? For how many years?"

"Ten at least," was the answer. "He came down to the Street when he was twenty. He was with Dunscomb & Fiske in 1893, I remember."

"The Street?" repeated the Count, questioningly.

"Yes, Wall Street. You knew he was a Wall Street stock broker, didn't you?"

The Chancellor paled perceptibly, his eyes widened a trifle and the straight line of his lips narrowed under his close-cropped moustache.

"Yes," he returned, diplomatically, after an instant's pause. "Yes. His name, I think, was Grey, was it not?"

"Grey. Yes, Carey Grey."

Count von Ritter cleared his throat and then for a moment he sat in silence, his lids half-closed, his mouth tight-drawn. When he spoke it was very seriously, with a changed demeanour.

"Budavia has still more for which to thank you, Mr. Van Tuyl," he said, rising.

The New York banker and the Irish lieutenant also stood up. It was evident to both that a blunder had been made.

"I don't just see for what," said the older man, a little nervously. "I haven't told you anything you didn't know. I didn't come here to tell you anything. I came to have you tell me something."

"I think," replied the Count, with an urbanity that was the acme of trained diplomacy, "that you said just now you came here to confirm a rumour, or words to that effect. You have, my dear sir, confirmed it. And now I must ask you to excuse me. You are at the Königin Anna, I suppose? I shall have the pleasure of calling upon you tomorrow."

The Chancellor bowed, smiling, and before Van Tuyl could remonstrate had disappeared into the Hall of Council. And then it was that O'Hara for the first time found words.

"Well, I'm damned!" he said. And he said it with emphasis.

Meanwhile the Colonial Secretary had finished his wearying oration and the Prince Regent had suggested the advisability of adjournment. But the return of the Chancellor, craving the privilege of the floor, awakened a new interest. His usually immobile face was portentous in its marked gravity, and when he spoke every ear was alert.

"Your Highness," he began, addressing the Prince Regent, "I am come to cry 'Pause!' I have listened to and taken part in a debate this evening the sole purpose of which, as I regard it now, has been to accomplish our own convincing. We constructed a theory upon a basis as unstable as the sands of the sea, and then marshalled arguments of straw to effect its establishment. In the whole history of Budavia I know of no incident of parallel puerility. We call ourselves statesmen, and we have acted with the confiding innocence of children. We gambolled like foolhardy lads blindfold upon the brink of a precipice, over which, had not a miracle intervened, we must have fallen into the slough of ignominious dishonour. Even as it is the smirch of its miasma is upon us, and we cannot escape the ridicule that is entailed.

"Our supposed mad Prince Maximilian of Kronfeld, now so carefully guarded in the Flag Tower, your Highness, is, I make bold to announce, a perfectly sane American gentleman and nothing more."

The Prince Regent leaned suddenly forward, his hands clutching the arms of his chair. The other members of the Council stirred, changed their positions; two of them got onto their feet. But the Chancellor still standing, the Prince Regent motioned them back to their places, and the speaker continued:

"In the chain of evidence I have, within the past five minutes, found a broken link. The statements made to me by the supposed heir have, in one important particular, been verified to my entire satisfaction, and these statements were, as you know, at utter variance with what we had been led to believe was the truth—in direct contradiction to the alleged proofs of royal birth."

"But, your Excellency," protested the Secretary for Foreign Affairs, rising again, "is not this simply jumping from one conclusion to another?"

The Chancellor frowned grimly.

"At first glance," he replied, resting the tips of his long, knotted fingers on the table between them, "it may appear so. But a chain is only as strong as its weakest link, and this link, as I have stated, has been shattered into infinitesimal atoms."

Count von Ritter spoke for fully an hour. He reviewed the affair from the beginning, detailing every step in the building up of the fabric and demonstrating with marked effect how a single pin-prick had brought about its total collapse. The pretender—if he could be so called in view of the fact that he personally had laid no claim to the throne, but, on the other hand, had of his own free will protested against the honour they would have forced upon him—should be quietly deported, and as expeditiously as possible arrangements effected for the coronation of Prince Hugo. The detection and punishment of those involved in the plot to steal the crown must be brought about with all the secrecy possible. Already two of the conspirators, he announced, were under arrest, and the apprehension of others would speedily follow.

It was long after midnight when the Council adjourned, and the Chancellor returned to his ancient mansion on the Graf Strasse. Rest for him, however, was not yet to come. Upon the writing table in his library were many State papers demanding his attention, and, aided by his secretary, who had been awaiting his home-coming, he went systematically to work to clear away the more important before retiring.

At a quarter past two he threw down his quill and leaned back in his chair with a yawn.

"That will do for tonight, Heinrich," he said, kindly, "I'm sorry to have had to keep you up so long."

And as he spoke the telephone rang long, loud and viciously. The secretary put the receiver to his ear, and answered into the mouthpiece. The Count rose and stretched himself. It was unusual for the telephone to ring at that hour, and he wondered, watching Heinrich's face. He saw the young man's chin drop and his eyes suddenly grow round.

"Your Excellency!" he exclaimed, excitement in his voice. "Your Excellency! Listen! The Crown Prince has escaped from the Flag Tower, together with his servant and Captain Lindenwald. And the Captain's man has been shot, seriously—they think fatally. One of the guards was found bound in His Royal Highness's apartment. Another guard has a broken leg, and three others are slightly injured."

XIX

THE following day was rife with revelations. Grey and Johann had arrived at the farmhouse of Herr Fahler before cock-crow and had been greeted first with a yelping of dogs and then by a cheery, if somewhat sleepy, welcome from the master of the house, to whom Minna had told the whole wonderful story. Johann he had recognised at once, and he had suspected the identity of his companion at sight. From a great cask in the corner of the big living-room he had drawn them foaming beakers of beer, and from a cupboard had produced for their further refreshment some cold meat and dark bread. And as they ate and drank, Frau Fahler had appeared to add her welcome to her husband's, and a little later the Fraülein, with rosy cheeks fresh from slumber and wearing the most becoming of negligées, had enthusiastically thrown her arms about Grey's neck and mingled tears of joy with her smiles over "Uncle Max's" deliverance.

At daybreak the fugitive Crown Prince wrote a note to Hope, telling her of his flight and his place of refuge, and one of the farm hands was despatched with it to the town. Then Minna suggested that the two refugees needed rest, and was for sending them to bed for a few hours' sleep, but Grey protested and Johann blankly refused.

In the American's mind one desire was now dominant—to see the contents of the late Herr Schlippenbach's luggage, among which, he was impressed, he would find some clue to the mystery—some evidence, perhaps, that would make clear what was still the most perplexing of enigmas. Whether this impression was born of hope, merely, or whether it was inspired by some psychic manifestation cannot be demonstrated and is not material; but, as the discoveries of the day proved, it was well founded.

After the family breakfast, which was served early, Minna took Grey to an upper room where were the three boxes of her great-uncle, and producing the keys a thorough search was made of the dead man's effects. In one box were his clothes, in another relics of his family, and in the third a small library of books and manuscripts, with many bottles and jars and boxes, wrapped in straw and packed with consummate care to guard against breakage.

The books for the most part bore on one subject—phrenology. Nearly every known work treating of it was included in the collection. There were the early writings of Dr. Franz Joseph Gall and his pupil, Dr. Spurzheim; there were the discoveries of George and Andrew Coombs and of Dr. Elliotson, and the lectures of that earliest and ablest of American phrenologists, Dr. Charles Caldwell, and of the later disciple, Fowler. All of these bore many annotations, marked paragraphs, underlined sentences and marginal comments. Here and there were inserted pages of closely written manuscript, recording the results of Schlippenbach's personal observation—cases that had come under his notice and to which he had given infinite study. From these it was very soon made apparent to Grey that the late Herr Doctor had ideas distinctively his own. While he accepted many of the conclusions of the earlier apostles of the creed he went a step further, and believed that character could be formed and developed by the systematic physical building up of certain portions of the mental structure and the depression of other portions. This, he claimed, was best accomplished by magnetic stimulation and absorption. Positive magnetic currents stimulated and nourished, while negative currents degenerated and destroyed.

He had conceived this theory, his writings made clear, while tutor at the Budavian Court, and had presumed to experiment on the infant Crown Prince. At that time he had kept a journal in which he made entry, briefly and roughly, not only of his scientific accomplishments, but of incidents bearing in any way on his career. This journal was secured by a lock, but Minna and her sister not merely consented to its breaking, but insisted upon it. And here was found the long and well-kept secret of the writer's quarrel with Queen Anna and the abduction of the young heir apparent. Her Majesty having been informed of the tutor's novel methods of mental development had commanded their cessation so far as her infant son was concerned; and the tutor's departure from the Court was only a part of the outcome. The journal revealed the fact—though it was not stated in so many words, and to those unfamiliar with Budavian history the entries might have meant nothing—that the tutor was, if not personally the abductor of the young sprig of royalty, certainly an important factor in the abduction, his object being not so much to avenge himself on Queen Anna as to gather the results of the experiments he had been engaged in from the child's earliest infancy. There was no direct mention, either, of the little fellow's death, but the absence after a few months of entries concerning him was good ground for the belief that he did not long survive his arrival in America.

Package after package of letters from Professor Trent showed that from the time of Schlippenbach's emigration up to almost the immediate present he had been in correspondence with the head of the University of Kürschdorf. In view of what Count von Ritter had told him, the more recent of these letters were to Grey of paramount interest, and he read them with careful attention, and especially one in which appeared the following paragraph:

You can fancy the surprise, not unmixed with joy, with which I read your letter of the twenty-fifth of August. The fact that the heir to our throne is still alive and where you can lay your hands upon him seems a wonderful dispensation of an all-wise Providence; for in the event of His Majesty's death—and he has been for two years a terrible sufferer from an incurable ailment—the crown must otherwise go, as you know, to that prince of scapegraces, Hugo. I have given your communication to the Chancellor, and you will doubtless hear from him in the near future. Fancy our future King, all unmindful, serving in the capacity of a valet! Truth is indeed stranger than fiction.

Subsequent letters gave hints here and there of the progress of the investigation, which, it seemed, was conducted with no little secrecy. From these it appeared that Schlippenbach had had many interviews with the Budavian Minister at Washington and the Budavian Consul at New York, but that the person of the pretended Crown Prince was not revealed to them until some time in March, by which date, or, in fact, as early as January, he had become a member of Schlippenbach's household in Avenue A. Of his removal from where he was supposed to have been in service to the home of the old Herr Doctor, Professor Trent wrote:

And you have not told him yet, you say, of the honours that are his. All through this I can see the Divine Hand. The embezzlement and disappearance of his employer offered just the opportunity you desired to have him with you. You can now, by degrees, fit him—gradually prepare him, I mean—for the high estate which is his inheritance; whereas had he continued in his employment such a procedure would have been hedged around with difficulties. I am glad you set me right in the matter of names. I knew that he had gone by the name of Lutz; and I could not understand who this other Lutz was. You say he is his foster-brother, the son of the woman who reared him. I think it wise to have him take another name for the journey over here; and your idea of having him pose as your nephew, Arndt, is capital, provided, of course, there is none of your nephews' friends or acquaintances coming on the same steamer.

The insight which these letters gave to Grey only served to whet his appetite for additional detail. Many of the revelations were startling, some of them in a way amusing, yet the general impression they made was not of the cleverness of the schemers but rather of their want of skill, their rash indiscretion, their apparently laboured complication of things, which by very reason of the resultant network offered unnecessary loopholes for discovery and frustration. In this he found proof of Schlippenbach's lack of balance, which he was charitable enough to consider the result of mental derangement. He was not so much a knave, he told himself, as he was a maniac.

From Kürschdorf the news had come to him that the King was going to die. He remembered then, possibly with a stricken conscience, that he was partly if not wholly responsible for the fact that His Majesty would leave no son to succeed him. If at this juncture he were able to produce the heir, what might he not expect in the way of honours? But the Crown Prince was dead and therefore not producible.

Grey could read very clearly between the lines of the story as it was opened up to him, and he perceived the birth just here of the temptation to produce the heir to the throne by constructing a replica of the deceased Maximilian. Had he been going about such a business himself, he would probably have chosen some conscienceless fellow to personify the departed one. But with Schlippenbach his science was always pre-eminent. As, years before, he had endeavoured by means of this to build up from the real infant heir a prince that should meet his views of what a prince should be, so now he chose to make, from a young man possessed of certain fitting physical and mental attributes, a prince to order.

The raw material must be tall, erect and of dignified bearing, of intelligence and education. The Crown Prince had been dark-eyed, but flaxen-haired. To secure this latter natural combination was not easy. But while his knowledge of chemicals left him powerless to change blue eyes to brown, his familiarity with the potency of peroxide of hydrogen made it quite possible for him to change black hair to blond. And so he set about finding a gentleman of the desired type. Daily he must have passed hundreds on the street, but seeing them and getting them within the radius of his ministration were two different things. In his circle of acquaintances he knew of no one that would answer. But from one of his acquaintants, Lutz, the valet, he had heard much of the valet's employer, and the valet's employer evidently seemed to him to be very nearly what he required.

All this Grey gathered by the very simple process of logical reasoning from what he found in Herr Schlippenbach's books and papers. But there was much still which by no method of inference could he satisfactorily explain.

In the examination of the contents of the boxes Minna was deeply interested, and with her Grey discussed each and every significant paragraph and passage. They were still busy exchanging views when, towards five o'clock in the afternoon, the sound of carriage wheels on the driveway below drew the Fraülein to the open window.

"Oh, dear," she cried, joyously, "it's Miss Van Tuyl and Mr. O'Hara and another gentleman. Come, we'll go down and meet them."

But Grey was not altogether pleased. In his note to Hope he had warned her that it would not be safe for her or anyone to visit or communicate with him until events shaped themselves one way or another. It being known that she and O'Hara had come to Kürschdorf with him they would probably be watched with a view to discovering his whereabouts. Seeing that he had sent this caution it was, he thought, most inconsiderate of them to disregard it. But he got up from his seat on the floor and went downstairs with

Minna, nevertheless; and in spite of his momentary annoyance there was only gladness in his eyes when they fell upon the brown-eyed, white-clad girl in the victoria, whose face was radiant with the joy of seeing him again and the good news that she was bringing. For she had not disobeyed, after all. Events had already shaped themselves, as her father's little speech—once introductions were over and they were all seated in the big square living-room—very definitely proved.

"I'm more than glad to see you, Carey, my boy," Nicholas Van Tuyl had exclaimed, gripping Grey's hand with a cordiality that was stimulating, "I'm delighted; and I'm happy to be the one to bring you the best news you have had in a long while." This had been said outside, and it had filled Grey with delicious expectancy. What followed, however, was even better than he imagined.

"Not an hour ago," began the New York banker, "I had a call from your friend, Chancellor von Ritter. I know him, met him in Munich years ago, and went to him last night to get the truth about your imprisonment. He wouldn't tell me anything then, but I told him enough, it seems, to upset the whole Privy Council and put a scapegrace on the throne of Budavia. However, that's only by way of introduction. This afternoon he called on me at the hotel, and told me a good many things that the great and glorious Budavian public will never know. He told me, for instance, how the Government had been fooled and how now it was going to get out of its predicament with as good a grace as possible. He told me all about your escape last night, and how you had done the very thing that he could have most wished. One of the problems that confronted him was how to get rid of you without revealing the Government's error. Now that you have taken the matter in your own hands, that question is answered. All he hopes is that they'll never be able to find you; and they won't—because they are going to shut their eyes and not look."

Grey laughed, and the rest of the party joined in.

"This diplomacy reminds me of a French farce," remarked O'Hara. "The actors who really know it all better than anyone else are apparently the only ones who cannot see what is perfectly palpable to the audience."

"If I were you," Van Tuyl continued, "I'd shave off that beard and moustache at once; that will make their dissembling appear a little bit real. And then I'd get out of town just as soon as I could make it convenient. Not that there would be any danger from the Government as it now stands, but with Hugo and his followers in command you can't tell what might happen overnight."

Grey nodded.

"Yes," he agreed, smiling, "I think you're right. I won't stop for the royal obsequies. It may seem disrespectful to my late sire, but now that I have my wings back I feel like using them."

"I never did care much for funerals," added Nicholas Van Tuyl, "and so Hope and I will go with you."

O'Hara's eyes were fixed on Minna, who was gazing pensively at the white-scrubbed floor.

"I think I'll stop," he said, a little seriously. "You won't need me, Grey, and I'd like to look over the Budavian military, which will be out in force."

The Fraülein's gaze was lifted and her eyes for an instant met those of the Irish lieutenant. In them he read the answer he craved to the question his heart was asking.

XX

GREY had set apart the books and papers that had to do either directly or indirectly with his case, because he saw in them a circumstantial defence to the charges which were still hanging over him at home. To his use of them for this purpose Minna and her sister gladly consented, and so when that evening, after having been cropped and clean-shaven by Johann, he bade the little household good-bye and was driven into town to the Grand Hotel Königin Anna, he carried this evidence with him.

It was, as has been observed, a day rife with revelations. The discoveries of its daylight hours were of incalculable value, but the disclosures reserved for the night were of even more consequence. The train that afternoon had brought from Paris a large company of visitors intent upon viewing the pomp and panoply of a royal funeral, and among them were the remaining members of that gay little dinner party at Armenonville the week before.

The Van Tuyls ran into them at the hotel on their return from the Fahler farm, and Hope immediately had an inspiration.

"I'm going to give a dinner tonight," she said, "just the most informal sort of a dinner in our *salon*. And I want you all to come. It doesn't make any difference whether you have your trunks or not. You are not expected to dress. I'm going to treat you to a surprise."

The women were all curiosity on the instant and showed it. The men accepted politely, but declared that the hostess was attraction sufficient.

Hope had made the proposition on impulse, and it was too late to draw back when she caught her father's disapproving eye.

"I'm not at all sure," he commented, once they were alone, "that this thing is wise. Carey isn't yet out of the woods, and the story of his alleged embezzlement and all that is too fresh to have been forgotten. Explanations at a dinner party aren't pleasant things. We know he is innocent, but you don't want to put him on trial before a jury of your guests."

But Hope was staunch in her loyalty.

"Our verdict will be sufficient," she answered, bravely. "If I had stopped to think of all you say I probably shouldn't have asked them, but as it is I'm glad I did it. It clears the situation at once. They must know from my having promised to be his wife and your having given your consent, that he is innocent."

Nicholas Van Tuyl shrugged his shoulders.

"Perhaps," he replied, a little doubtfully, "perhaps; but, my dear girl, don't hint at the Prince business. The Fahlers will keep their mouths closed for the sake of their dead relative, but no injunction of secrecy would still the tongues of Mrs. Dickie and Lady Constance."

Hope demurred.

"It's such an interesting story," she protested, "and I am a woman!"

"But the Government here does not want it to get out."

"And I'd like to know what we owe to the Government," the girl inquired. "I don't want to be disobedient, father dear, but I can't promise to control myself under provocation."

Again Mr. Van Tuyl shrugged his shoulders. His daughter was his idol and he was as yarn in her hands.

When Grey arrived and was told of the plan, he received the tidings somewhat ruefully. He complained that his trunks were still at the Residenz Schloss, and that, in the torn and bedraggled raiment he was wearing, to pose as the object of interest at a dinner party, no matter how informal, was apt to be a little trying, to say the least. But O'Hara, who had driven into town with him, came to the rescue. He and Grey were very nearly of a size, and as he was the fortunate possessor of two evening suits he promptly placed one of them at Grey's disposal.

Nevertheless, in spite of this satisfactory overcoming of a grave difficulty, Grey was not present when the party sat down to dinner; for, as he was about to join the company,

Nicholas Van Tuyl broke in upon him, carrying in his hand a note which had just been delivered by an orderly from the Royal Hospital.

"You'll have to go, won't you?" he asked, as Grey ran his eye over the page.

It was from Chancellor von Ritter and was addressed to the banker.

"If you are in communication with Mr. Grey," it read, "send him here with all speed. The man Lutz can last only a few hours. He is anxious to make an ante-mortem statement, but insists that Mr. Grey shall be present when he makes it."

And so Grey rushed off in a cab, and as the dinner party took their places at table in the Van Tuyl *salon*, he was climbing the Royal Hospital stairs to the little white room in which lay dying the young man who had served him faithfully for over two years as valet, only to fall by reason of avarice into the rôle of villain in his life's melodrama.

The eyes that looked up at him from dark, cavernous depths in a face pale as chalk had in them an appeal that touched a chord of his sympathy, and for the moment he forgot the injuries he had suffered and remembered only the services he had experienced at those hands, which lay limp and waxen-yellow against the spotless white of the coverlet.

The small room was somewhat crowded. Chancellor von Ritter was there with a notary and a stenographer; near the window stood a soldier, whose very presence seemed an irony, which he appeared to recognise in retiring as far as the limits of the tiny chamber would permit; and there, too, of course, was the inevitable nun-like nurse in significantly immaculate muslin and the great flaring headdress of her sisterhood.

"He seems a little stronger at the moment," whispered the Chancellor; "you came at an opportune time. He has been asking for you all the afternoon."

The nurse was moistening the sufferer's lips. When she finished, Grey spoke to him.

"I am sorry to see you here, Lutz," he said, simply.

His breathing, he noticed, was very short and laboured.

"I'm obliged to you for coming, sir," he replied, and his voice was stronger than one would have expected. "I've got a lot to tell you; but it's so late now I don't know whether I'll be able." He paused between his sentences in an effort to husband his waning strength. "I was a good enough fellow once, Mr. Grey, wasn't I?"

Grey nodded.

"Yes," he agreed, with sincerity, "you were all right, Lutz."

"I never really meant you any harm, sir," he went on. "It seemed to me that it would be a good thing for you."

The Chancellor motioned to the stenographer, who drew his chair closer to the bedside and took a note-book and pencil from his pocket.

"Afterwards," Lutz continued, "after Dr. Schlippenbach died and I knew we couldn't keep you under the spell any more, I got frightened; and then I drank a good deal, and I—yes, I was crazy at times. Absinthe, Mr. Grey. I wasn't used to it, and it turned my head. I thought to save myself I must get rid of you. I tried to smother you with gas that night last week in Paris. Captain Lindenwald knew of it. He was afraid of you, too. He said suspicion would fall on Baron von Einhard; that we would never be suspected. And when I failed he went to Baron von Einhard and—how much he got I don't know; but the Baron paid him to go away and leave you, agreeing that he would put you where you would never be heard of again. Then we came here, with a story about your being mad and being locked up in a Paris sanitarium. It was the only thing we could do. If the plan had worked we should have been in trouble for a while, maybe, but when Prince Hugo came to the throne we should have been rewarded. I sold the Baron the strong-box with all those manufactured proofs of your right to the crown; and I told him you had the Prince of Kronfeld ring. I'm sorry, sir, I'm sorry. But I'm a coward, and I was in terror and more than half insane with that green stuff."

"Yes, yes, I know," Grey interjected. "But tell me, Lutz, how this whole thing started, back in New York. Tell me about Schlippenbach and how you and he managed it together."

The nurse, from her place by the pillow, leaned over and wiped her patient's brow. Then she moistened his lips again, and his deep-sunken eyes looked his appreciation. For some minutes he was silent, endeavouring apparently by an effort of will to gather fresh energy; and to Grey's mind recurred the picture of that darkened room in Paris, just six days ago, with the dying Herr Schlippenbach struggling to make himself understood.

"He was more devil than man," Lutz resumed. "He was always working with strange drugs and experimenting with batteries on cats and dogs, and children, too. One day he asked me a great many questions about you, Mr. Grey, and then he asked me if I'd like to be rich—very rich, he said. 'Everyone wants to be rich,' I answered. 'If you'll do just as I tell you,' he said, 'you'll have more money than you ever dreamed of.' He told me he wanted me to put just one tiny pellet in your coffee each morning. It would not harm you, he said, but you would doze off for just ten minutes after you had taken it, and you would never know you had been dozing. 'And while he is asleep,' he said, 'you can tell him to do anything you wish at any time in that day and he will do it. Tell him, for instance,' he advised me, 'to double your wages when he returns from his office in the evening, and he will do it.' I laughed at the idea and had no faith in it; but I consented to try it. And it worked. You did double my wages, Mr. Grey, just as I asked you to, and you never knew I had asked you. Each day I gave you the pellet, as he directed, and each day I suggested that you do certain things at certain hours, and you always did them."

"Hypnotic suggestion," commented Grey, involuntarily.

"Something like it," Lutz replied, "but he said it was not. At least, only in part. The pellet was the principal thing. He made the pellets himself. They were his secret. I gave you the last the day before he died; and I knew then that I could control you no more."

"Yes," Grey urged, "but after the first, what happened? After I raised your wages, what other things did you suggest?"

"Nothing of importance for a month or two. Just trifles—that you come home early and tell me you would not require me that night; or that you would give me a coat I wanted very much, and things of that sort. But one day

Schlippenbach came to the rooms while you were down town. 'Tomorrow morning,' he said,'I am coming here early, before Mr. Grey is up. You must hide me somewhere until you have given him the pellet.' He came and I hid him in your wardrobe; but when you had had your coffee with his drug in it he came out, and then I saw for the first time the power of this thing. He directed you very minutely and very exactly. Every minute in the day you were under his commands. You were to secure a hundred thousand dollars in cash and you were to bring it to his house on Avenue A at four o'clock in the afternoon. And at this house you were to remain. That evening I went there, and there you were. You did not know me. Your name had been changed to Arndt. I called you Mr. Grey to test the thing, and you appeared to think I was crazy. Schlippenbach told me you had brought the money. You never left his house until we sailed for this country."

"What did I do there?"

"You did very little, but Schlippenbach did a great deal. Each day he had his batteries working on your head. He told me he was building up your self-esteem and that he was depleting your reverence. He was developing those cerebral organs which he thought would fit you for a throne and reducing those which he thought would unfit you. He said that in this way he could change you completely. After a few years of constant treatment, three or four years at most, you would, he told me, be no more Mr. Grey, the New York broker, than I would. You would be the King of Budavia and never know that you had not been born to it. And then there would be no further need of pellets or of galvanism. The transformation would have been accomplished."

The dying man, becoming more and more interested in his subject, was speaking in clearer tones and with much less effort; and his auditors listened, spellbound, to his exposition of the marvellous methods of his mountebank master.

"And as the days went on it was wonderful how you did change, sir. You spoke differently and you acted differently. He made you grow a beard and moustache, which he bleached without your knowledge, as he did your hair, and your most intimate friend wouldn't have recognised you, Mr. Grey. I don't believe your mother would have known you, sir."

"And the money?" Grey queried, fearing that in his enthusiasm Lutz would overtax his strength and leave this most important point uncovered. "What did Schlippenbach do with the hundred thousand dollars?"

"A good deal of it was spent," the valet answered, "but some of it is still in the East River National Bank, and some with Graeff & Welbrock, the German bankers. When we came away we brought with us two letters of credit, one in his name and one in yours, for twenty thousand dollars each."

Of these facts Grey made a mental note.

"Some of it you will get back, sir," Lutz added, after a pause. "Perhaps most of it, for the old man owns some property on the East Side, and you can prove that he was responsible for the theft. And now, Mr. Grey"—and something in the nature of a smile flickered ghastly and distressful about the corners of his livid mouth—"I think I have told you all. But"—his yellow right hand slid slowly a few inches over the coverlet towards its edge—"I have in return a favour to ask. Maybe you'll feel you can't grant it. I'm going pretty fast, I imagine. They say I won't last till daylight comes, and—I'd like, sir—if you don't mind too much"—his sentences were very halt once more—"don't mind too much——"

Grey leaned over and took the sliding hand in his own.

"All right, Lutz," he said, with a tremour in his voice that he could not control, "all right, man. I don't believe you were half to blame. He had you under a spell, too, I dare say. I forgive you freely, and God bless you!"

The flickering, vagrant smile merged into an expression of peace. Into the sunken eyes came resignation.

"Thank you, sir!" the grey lips murmured, "thank you! thank you!"

The notary mumbled a form of oath to which Lutz gave a voiceless assent. Then his lids fell, and when Grey and Count von Ritter left the room he was barely conscious.

"I'll have a certified copy of the statement sent to you Mr. Grey," the Chancellor volunteered. "In it you will have evidence that is beyond all dispute. I congratulate you on securing such a complete refutation of so baseless and yet so dangerous a slander."

XXI

THE contrast between the tiny white room in the hospital with the dire shadow of the Grim Reaper hovering over the narrow cot bed, and the spacious, brilliant *salon* of the hotel, where life, assertive, aggressive, almost obtrusive, was dominant, had something of a dazzling effect on Carey Grey, and he paused a moment on the threshold, with blinking eyes, in an effort to adjust his vision to the sudden change of scene.

There was a momentary lull in the merriment that smote him as the door swung open in answer to his knock, and then the cannonade of voices—of cries of surprise, of welcoming greetings, of laughter—was resumed, and Nicholas Van Tuyl rose from his place at the round table, which, with its snowy damask dotted with pink-shaded candles and dappled with silver and crystal, seemed like the centre of some giant flower of which the men and women about it were the variegated petals.

"My friends," cried the host, raising his voice and hand simultaneously for silence, "I have pleasure in presenting to you my future son-in-law, Mr. Carey Grey, of New York."

The next instant everybody was shouting at once. The men were up and bearing down on the newcomer in a solid phalanx, and Lady Constance and Mrs. Dickie were waving their napkins and fairly shrieking their congratulations. When at length something like order reigned again, Frothingham found his champagne glass and proposed a toast:

"To the bride-elect," he cried. "'She moves a goddess and she looks a queen.'"

Grey's response was brief but enthusiastic, and the significance of the quotation with which he closed it evoked an outburst of applause that must have been heard as far as the Kursaal, two blocks away.

"All yet seems well, and if it end so meet,
The bitter past, more welcome is the sweet.
The king's a beggar now the play is done:
All is well ended, if *this* suit be won."

He did not know it at the time, but prior to his coming the whole story of his adventure had been related and discussed, much to the entertainment of the party in general and to the intense edification and delight of young Edson in particular, who resolved to make to his chief, the Ambassador, a full report of the extraordinary affair, with a view to having it forwarded to Washington to be filed among the State archives, as indicative of a vulnerable point in Budavia's boasted supremacy in statecraft. The aptness of the quotation, therefore, was more generally appreciated than Grey had any notion it would be, and the hilarious approbation of his auditors was consequently a good deal of a surprise.

Nicholas Van Tuyl, however, leaned over in the midst of the cheering, to tell him that the plot of his play and the part he had enacted were known to the company. The news was not ungrateful, for from the moment of his entrance he had felt a natural restraint, which was now relieved. Very soon the matter came up again, and he related his experience at the hospital, which was listened to with the deepest interest.

"Under the circumstances," observed Sinclair Edson when Grey had finished, "it is not surprising that the extradition proceedings have been withdrawn."

"Withdrawn?" exclaimed Grey, in amazement. "If it be true I should say it were most surprising."

"We had a cable to that effect yesterday before I left Paris," continued the secretary. "They were withdrawn at the instance of your partner, Mr. Mallory."

"That is inexplicable," Grey commented. "He doesn't know anything more now than he did a week ago."

Van Tuyl drained his wine-glass and wiped his lips with his napkin.

"Oh, yes he does, Carey," he said, "he knows pretty much about it. I took the liberty of cabling to him all I knew. Besides, that whole business was a mare's nest. If you hadn't disappeared there would never have been any prosecution. Any one knows that a partner can't be held for borrowing from his own firm, and unless I'm very much mistaken you were in a position to turn over real estate worth several times the amount secured on the bonds."

"That is very true," Grey replied, smiling, "but, strange as it may seem, that view of the situation never occurred to me before."

"The newspapers were responsible for most of the hue and cry, I fancy," Van Tuyl continued, "and as for the extradition part, I imagine Mallory took that step more from an impulse to find out whether the cable you sent him was really from you, and with the hope of locating you—dragging you back from the grave, so to speak—than with an idea of punishment for a crime that was never really committed."

A Dresden clock on the mantel-shelf had tinkled midnight before the party broke up, agreeing to be down for an early breakfast at a quarter of eight, since the Van Tuyls and Grey were leaving Kürschdorf at nine, to connect with the Orient Express at Munich.

When the rest had gone, Grey, who had lingered, drew Hope out onto the balcony. The music of the band which had floated up from below throughout the evening had ceased, but the rushing Weisswasser and the breeze stirring the foliage of the trees on the Quai combined in a melody to which their hearts beat a joyous refrain. The stars twinkled in unison in the blue-black canopy of the heavens, and from the distance a nightingale's song made chorus.

"'She moves a goddess and she looks a queen,'" Grey repeated, his arm about the girl's supple waist. "That was an inspiration on Frothingham's part. The line was never more aptly quoted. *My* goddess! *My* queen! Ah, my darling, if I could only make you know the happiness that is mine tonight!"

Her head was resting against his shoulder, but now she turned her face to him and in her eyes was a world of passionate adoration.

"I know," she murmured, softly. "It is mine, too, dear. It is a mutual happiness, and we both know it. That is the reason it is so sweet."

He drew her still closer, until he could feel her heart beating against his side.

"God is good," he said, reverently. "There were moments in the past week when I saw only the frowning face of an implacable fate; when I felt that the net woven about me was too cruelly strong ever to give way to my struggles; and then I was more than half inclined to curse God and die. But we are only blind children, as it has been said, and when Providence is preparing for us the most delectable morsels we grow rebellious because we can't see just how it is being done."

"'More welcome is the sweet,'" she quoted, returning the pressure of his hand. "You will never know, my very dear, the agony I suffered in those weeks after your disappearance. I would have died gladly—oh, so gladly; but, as you say, God is good, only we cannot always see. The sky was very black, without a single star, and the sun would never rise again, never, never. I knew it."

"But it has, love, hasn't it?" Grey asked, cheerily. "And we'll pray now for a long, long, sunshiny day to make up for so dark a night."

Then he bent his head and kissed her; and the nightingale's song was a pæan, and the music of the trees and the river a serenade.

After a little, Nicholas Van Tuyl joined them.

"Well, lad," he said to Grey, as he flicked the ashes from his cigar, "what are your plans?"

"I'm taking *La Savoie* from Havre on Saturday," the young man answered. "I'd rather lose my right arm than leave Hope now, just as I have found her, but there's no getting out of it. I must hurry back to New York and square things."

"You must go so soon, dear?" she questioned, with just a suspicion of a pout.

"I must," he replied, reluctance in his voice. "I'll try to rejoin you later; but every duty demands my presence in America now."

"We'll have to stop, of course," Van Tuyl observed; and then he added, with a smile: "my daughter, here, will be very busy, I fancy, for the next few weeks with *couturières* and *marchandes de modes* in the rue de la Paix and thereabouts. So don't exercise yourself unnecessarily, Carey. She'll hardly have time to miss you. There's no salve in the world to a woman so effective as that to be found in ordering new finery."

"Don't you believe him, dear," the girl protested, her fingers tightening on Grey's hand. "I shall think of you every minute I'm awake, and dream of you every minute I'm asleep."

The two men lounging against the iron railing of the balcony smoked and chatted for a long time after Hope went in. They had much in common, and to each occurred a multiplicity of matters of mutual interest.

Meanwhile the street below grew quiet, the terrace was deserted, the wind in the trees died to a whisper, and the incessant murmur of the hurrying waters accentuated rather than disturbed the silence. But the two great lamps on either side of the hotel's broad entrance still blazed, throwing a half circle of illumination out across the roadway and in under the lindens of the Quai.

Grey, flinging away the end of his cigar, turned and looked down, watching it fall and sputter red sparks upon the macadam of the drive. And as he looked a shadow glided swiftly across the arc of light beneath the trees and was swallowed up in the gloom beyond—a shadow, the contour of which even in that brief moment struck Grey as unmistakably familiar, recalling a figure that he had seen twenty-four hours before, leaping wildly, from dark to dark, down a winding stone stairway.

"It's bed time," said Nicholas Van Tuyl, yawning. "You must be tired. Suppose we——"

A pistol shot, startlingly loud and sharp against the night silence, clipped off the end of the sentence.

For a moment neither spoke, and the stillness was the stillness of death. Then came the patter of hurrying steps, and presently voices were heard and men were darting across the street from all directions, and all heading toward the Quai at a point just opposite the balcony.

"Murder?" suggested Van Tuyl.

"No," answered Grey, with conviction. "Suicide."

Five minutes later, as they watched and listened, the crowd came straggling back, two by two and in groups, all chattering.

"Poor devil!" said one. The words rose distinctly audible.

"He made very sure," commented another.

"Fancy blowing out his brains on the edge of the Quai and burying himself in the river!" exclaimed a third.

"For love, I suppose," a young man ventured.

"Lost his last mark at the Kursaal tonight probably," an older man theorised.

Grey and Van Tuyl turned into the *salon* through the open window.

"That is what is called retribution," said the younger man, "but it is usually longer delayed."

Van Tuyl's face asked for enlightenment.

"I could hardly have been mistaken," Grey answered, with assurance. "I saw the fellow just a moment before. It was Captain Lindenwald, of the Royal Household and Equerry to the late King Frederic of Budavia."

THE END

Milton Keynes UK
Ingram Content Group UK Ltd.
UKHW040817051024
449151UK00004B/280